T0043476

Beginner's guide to WEIGHT LIFTING

Beginner's *guide to* WEIGHT LIFTING

Simple Exercises and Workouts to Get Strong

KYLE HUNT

callisto
publishing
an imprint of Sourcebooks

Copyright © 2020 by Callisto Publishing LLC
Cover and internal design © 2020 by Callisto Publishing LLC
Illustrations by © Charlie Layton; Christian Papazoglakis, p.10.
All photography used under license from iStock.com.
Interior and Cover Designer: Sean Doyle
Art Producer: Sara Feinstein
Editor: Gleni Bartels
Production Editor: Andrew Yackira

Callisto and the colophon are registered trademarks of Callisto Publishing LLC.

All rights reserved. No part of this book may be reproduced in any form or by any electronic or mechanical means including information storage and retrieval systems—except in the case of brief quotations embodied in critical articles or reviews—without permission in writing from its publisher, Sourcebooks LLC.

All brand names and product names used in this book are trademarks, registered trademarks, or trade names of their respective holders. Callisto Publishing is not associated with any product or vendor in this book.

Published by Callisto Publishing LLC C/O Sourcebooks LLC
P.O. Box 4410, Naperville, Illinois 60567-4410
(630) 961-3900
callistopublishing.com

Printed and Bound In China
OGP 20

To my beautiful wife, Ashlyn, without whom this could not have been possible.

CONTENTS

INTRODUCTION

WE ALL START as beginners. My weight lifting journey began during my teenage years. I think I am part of the last generation heavily influenced by Sylvester Stallone, Arnold Schwarzenegger, and other film action heroes of the late '80s and early '90s. From the first day I picked up a weight following my eighth-grade wrestling season, I was hooked!

The word "passion" is thrown around a lot, but no other word describes my love for lifting weights. Studying exercise science in college was a no-brainer. The truth is, without lifting weights, I'm not sure what I would be doing with my life.

Over the past 10 years I have worked with hundreds of clients from all walks of life to prevent them from making the same mistakes I did. When I started out, I wasted a lot of time following bad advice. Without a knowledge of fundamentals, it can be hard to know who to trust. I want this book to be a resource that provides enough information to get you started on the right path.

Like other forms of exercise, such as cardio or yoga, weight lifting offers a wide range of benefits. Unlike other forms, however, it specializes in the use of resistance, or load, to induce muscular contraction that builds strength, mobility, endurance, and the size of skeletal muscles.

To make sure this book is helpful to beginners, it starts from square one. If you have some experience with weight lifting, some information contained here might be familiar to you. Even so, a recommitment to the basics is never a bad idea!

WHY WEIGHT LIFTING?

Although the common perception is that weight lifting is only for meathead bodybuilders and powerlifters, there are many other benefits of lifting weights that go beyond having big muscles. Don't get me wrong, this book will discuss how lifting weights helps you get fit and look great, but there are also holistic health benefits to lifting weights.

A HEALTHIER HEART: A study in *Medicine & Science in Sports & Exercise* shows that lifting weights can lower bad cholesterol and reduce blood pressure. Strength training can reduce the risk of heart attack, stroke, or death related to heart disease. Even lifting weights for less than an hour a week may reduce your risk for a heart attack or stroke by 40 to 70 percent.

STRONGER BONES: As we age, we lose muscle strength, mobility, coordination, and bone density. Lifting weights helps prevent all those issues. Physical activity, particularly weight lifting, has been shown to provide the mechanical stimuli, or "loading," important for the maintenance and improvement of bone health. This is particularly an issue for women across their lifespans, as it reduces the risk of osteoporosis.

BETTER MENTAL HEALTH: In addition to boosting your self-confidence and self-esteem, strength training has positive effects on mental health: Symptoms of depression and anxiety are reduced—and sleep is improved, which has a direct effect on mental health.

INCREASED METABOLISM: "Metabolism" basically refers to the amount of energy (calories) we burn each day. A sluggish metabolism makes it hard to lose weight and keep it off long term. Strength training doesn't just burn calories, it also increases lean muscle mass, which stimulates your metabolism. Lean muscle mass increases the amount of calories you need to maintain your weight and also makes it easier for you to exercise harder, which increases caloric expenditure.

INCREASED FLEXIBILITY AND BALANCE: Flexibility and balance are crucial elements of daily living we take for granted, but they become increasingly important as we age to help reduce falls and injuries. A loss of muscle mass contributes to decreased flexibility and balance, so maintaining your muscle mass is important to your stability. Lifting weights can help you move your joints through a full range of motion, which also helps maintain flexibility.

WHY THIS BOOK?

Although there are many books on the market that cover the topic of weight lifting, this book is specifically written with the beginner in mind—starting from the ground up and emphasizing fundamentals. No matter your age or ability, it's never too late to start lifting weights!

Even before stepping foot in the gym, we will go over all the common weight lifting jargon and explain all relevant gym equipment. If preventive measures are taken, weight lifting is an incredibly safe activity. To give you the best foundation, there is a detailed guide reviewing proper form with tips to avoid injury.

Good nutrition goes hand in hand with a solid weight lifting routine. To get the most out of your training, it's important to develop good nutritional habits. To help you, I break down nutrition into only the most important aspects so you won't be overwhelmed with "rules" and misinformation.

In part three it all comes together with weight lifting routines to start your training journey. The four-week program includes specific exercises, sets, reps, and tips on how to modify the exercises for your ability level. Even the gym-centric exercises give you an option to do them at home.

PART ONE

GETTING STARTED

THE BEST WAY to change your life is to improve your health and fitness. Starting a weight lifting program is an excellent way to accomplish that goal. As a beginner, it can be hard to know where to start, so this section covers the fundamentals of a weight lifting routine. Jargon is demystified, myths debunked, and a lot of time will be spent reviewing the safest ways to exercise and avoid injury so weight lifting can become a sustainable part of your everyday life.

CHAPTER 1

WEIGHT LIFTING 101

For most people, the hardest part of going to the gym is physically *going* to the gym. Starting a weight lifting routine from zero can be daunting, especially when it can feel like the gym is full of extremely fit people who all know what they're doing. This section is your crash course on all aspects of weight lifting. After reading this, you should be able to pick up a weight or walk through those gym doors confidently.

BEFORE YOU BEGIN

Everyone responds to training differently. As cliché as it might sound, it's important to focus on yourself and your personal progress. The famous Theodore Roosevelt quote, "Comparison is the thief of joy," is definitely applicable to fitness. Remember, you're not in competition with others at the gym. Genetics play a big role in how we build muscle, gain strength, lose fat, and respond to weight lifting in general. People progress in their weight lifting journeys at different rates. Consistency and progression are important.

Not every exercise in this book will be right for you from the start. We all have unique limb lengths, muscle insertions (the end of a muscle that attaches to the bone joint), and body types; there are many factors that make some exercises more effective than others. At their most basic, exercises are just tools you can use to build a routine that works for you. In the exercise section (page 33), you will find plenty of modifications to make sure the program meets you where you are in your fitness journey.

As always, consult your physician or qualified health care professional on any matter regarding your health before starting a new workout or fitness routine.

HOW WEIGHT LIFTING WORKS

The science of weight lifting and how muscles work can best be described as a three-step process of stimulus, recovery, and adaptation.

The process starts in the gym with a **stimulus** (a workout). Immediately after the workout, the body's **recovery** systems begin to heal and rebuild the tissue damaged by the workout. Although lifting weights sets the stage for progress, you don't build muscle or gain strength while you're training. In fact, when you finish a session and your body begins to heal itself, your muscle size and strength are actually reduced.

It's common to feel muscle soreness 24 to 48 hours after a weight lifting workout. This is called delayed onset muscle soreness, DOMS for short, and it happens while your muscles heal. Once the recovery occurs, so do the desired **adaptations**—muscles! This is why it's important to take rest days, to fully recover and heal, and not push your body past its limits.

IDENTIFY YOUR GOALS

I want to stress the importance of good habits for long-term success, especially when it comes to your weight lifting goals. There is no doubt goal setting is important; however, the difference between those who create goals and those who achieve them comes down to developing consistent habits.

Here are some examples of the types of weight lifting goals you might set:

BUILDING MUSCLE: The desire to build muscle is what first leads many people to pick up a weight. Building lean muscle mass will affect your appearance and body composition. It's a long-term investment, as maintaining muscle mass is important for maintaining a high quality of life as we age.

GAINING STRENGTH: When you first start lifting weights, you actually gain strength before you gain new muscle, so don't be fooled by appearances. You can improve your absolute strength (how much you can lift for one rep) or relative strength (how much you can lift relative to your body weight).

IMPROVING CARDIOVASCULAR HEALTH: When people think of cardiovascular health, they often think of traditional cardio exercises such as running or biking, but weight lifting has been shown to have a greater impact on reducing heart-related risks.

Track Your Progress

Keeping track of your progress is an important part of your weight lifting journey. Seeing your improvements in a tangible way is key to staying motivated. Below are two of my favorite, easy ways to record your headway.

Keep a workout journal or log

Keeping a workout journal is one of the simplest and most effective ways to track progress. One of the biggest mistakes people make in the gym is using the same amount of weight week after week. Over time, the body adapts to lifting weights. If you do the same thing over and over, your body stops responding. The goal is to *increase* the amount of weight you lift over time.

How much weight you lift is not the only thing to track. It's also a good idea to jot down the date, the specific exercises, the number of sets/reps, how heavy or light the weight felt, and what time the workout started and ended. Although I just use an old-school composition notebook because it is quick and easy, you may choose to use an app, like Strong Workout Tracker Gym Log (iPhone) or FitNotes (Android). There are many apps that provide training programs, but you want one that provides tracking ability.

Test yourself

Once every four to six weeks, test your strength on various lifts. You can do this any number of ways, but the simplest is to work up to the heaviest weight you can safely lift with good form. Each workout, compare your progress to the previous one.

Weight Lifting Myths: Fact or Fiction

We live in an amazing time! With just a quick Google search, you can pretty much learn anything you want. However, it's important to make sure the information you find is actually true. Some fitness myths refuse to go away, no matter how many times they've been disproven. Here are a few:

Lifting weights makes you "bulky": Men wish this myth were true, and it's one that many women worry about. The truth is, it's incredibly difficult to build enough muscle to look bulky. The muscle-building process takes time and requires a lot of consistent training. Getting "too big" certainly won't sneak up on you overnight, nor is it anything you need to worry about. The best way to get a lean, toned, muscular—not bulky—physique is by lifting weights.

Weight lifting is bad for the joints: Any exercise can be dangerous if done incorrectly. However, when done with proper form and appropriate weight, weight lifting is perfectly safe on the joints. In fact, when done correctly, lifting weights can improve joint mobility and stability, leading to long-term joint health.

You can crunch your way to a visible six-pack: One of the biggest myths in fitness is the idea of spot reduction. Unfortunately, you cannot lose fat from one specific area of the body by performing exercises for that body part. Although it's true that crunches help develop your abdominal muscles, to get a visible six-pack your body fat has to be low enough for them to show.

WEIGHT LIFTING JARGON DEFINED

When you walk into any gym for the first time it might seem as though everyone is speaking a foreign language. Let's go over some basic terms to translate that lingo. More terms are listed in the Glossary (page 131).

BARBELL: A barbell consists of a long bar, collars, sleeves, and associated plates. Barbells can be adjustable (allowing plates to be added or taken off) or fixed (the barbell is a nonadjustable weight). A standard Olympic barbell weighs 45 pounds.

BODYWEIGHT EXERCISE: Any exercise that uses your own bodyweight for resistance.

CABLE MACHINE: A machine with long cords attached to weight stacks at one end and a handgrip at the other.

COMPOUND EXERCISE: Any exercise that works more than one muscle group at a time, such as the squat and bench press.

DUMBBELL: Short bars on which weight plates are fixed and secured. Dumbbells can be considered a one-arm version of a barbell. Most dumbbells have their weight written on the side.

FLEXIBILITY: The range of motion possible at a joint, or the ability to use joints and muscles through their full range of motion.

FREQUENCY: This could refer to how often a movement is done in a week, how often a muscle group is trained in a week, or how often a workout is performed in a week.

ISOLATION EXERCISE: Any exercise aimed at working only one muscle group at a time, such as the biceps curl and leg extension.

MUSCULAR STRENGTH: The maximum amount of force a muscle can exert against some form of resistance in a single effort.

PROGRAM: Another word for routine, schedule, plan, etc. It refers to the complete number of sets, reps, and exercises performed on a given day.

PROGRESSIVE OVERLOAD: The gradual increase of stress placed upon the body during training.

PROPER FORM: A specific way of performing an exercise to avoid injury, prevent cheating, and increase effectiveness.

RANGE OF MOTION (ROM): The measurement of movement around a specific joint or body part. A "full range of motion" refers to the maximum amount of movement around a specific joint for a given exercise.

RECOVERY: The process of returning to a pre-exercise state.

REP: Short for "repetition," referring to one complete movement of an exercise, for example, squatting and standing back up is one rep.

REST PERIOD: The amount of time you take between each set of an exercise, typically, 1 to 3 minutes.

SET: The predetermined number of consecutive reps in a row is known as a set.

TRAINING TO FAILURE: Continuing a set until the muscle simply cannot contract to complete any additional reps.

WEIGHT PLATE: Varying sizes of circular iron weights placed on a barbell to add weight. Weight plates typically come in 2½ pounds, 5 pounds, 10 pounds, 25 pounds, 35 pounds, and 45 pounds.

WEIGHT LIFTING ROUTINE FUNDAMENTALS

As a beginner, having a well-organized, detailed plan is very important if you want to achieve the best results. Most beginners make the mistake of jumping into a workout routine that is too advanced. Part three (page 116) includes four weeks of detailed routines that take all the following into account so you can just focus on the exercises.

Here are a few basic elements of a well-constructed workout program:

DON'T NEGLECT THE WARM-UP: Skipping the warm-up is one of many mistakes I made as a novice lifter. The warm-up gets your body ready to optimally and safely perform the workout for the day.

STICK TO 60-MINUTE WORKOUTS: Each workout should last about 1 hour, including both the warm-up and cooldown. As a beginner, more is not always better.

PERFORM COMPOUND EXERCISES FIRST: From time and effectiveness standpoints, you will get the most bang for your buck by prioritizing compound movements. Exercises such as the squat, deadlift, row, and bench press work multiple muscles in one movement. Because these exercises are the most demanding, do them toward the beginning of the workout when you are fresh.

DON'T TRAIN THE SAME MUSCLES TWO DAYS IN A ROW: As a beginner, doing three full-body workouts per week is ideal. This allows adequate rest between each session, which ensures you won't be working the same muscle group on consecutive days. Remember, you don't actually build muscle or gain strength while in the gym. It's not until your body rests and recovers that those adaptations take place.

BUILD IN PROGRESSION: One key component of making progress is doing more work over time. Muscles need to be constantly challenged. If the same weights are used for the same number of reps, the muscles won't have any reason to adapt.

ALWAYS COOL DOWN: At the end of a long workout, take advantage of your warm muscles and work on flexibility with static stretches.

THE MAIN MUSCLE GROUPS

Here are the main muscle groups focused on in this training program. More detail on each muscle group is provided later in the book.

ABS AND CORE: While you're likely familiar with sit-ups, you'll also find additional exercises to work your midsection.

ARMS AND SHOULDERS: Your upper arm includes the biceps group and the triceps group, which actually forms the largest part of your upper arm. There are actually three muscles comprising your shoulder: the anterior, middle, and posterior deltoids.

BACK: To train and develop the musculature of your upper back, you'll use pulldowns and rows.

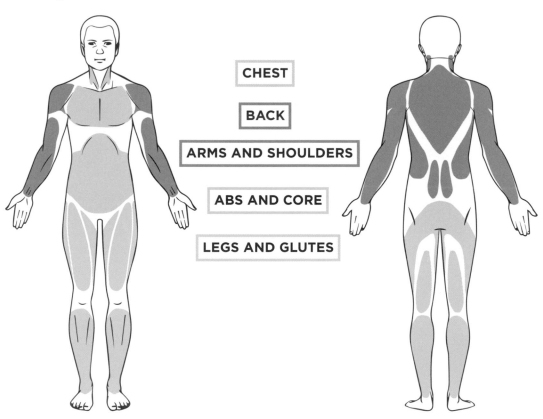

CHEST

BACK

ARMS AND SHOULDERS

ABS AND CORE

LEGS AND GLUTES

CHEST: When people think of chest training, the first thing that usually comes to mind is the bench press, and for good reason. The bench press is one of the best chest movements you can do.

LEGS AND GLUTES: If you're moving, you're using your legs. Lifting your children, walking to the car or around the block, taking an early-morning jog, and even balancing rely on a strong lower body. Developing strength in your legs and glutes will help you throughout the day.

Weight Lifting and Cardio

Cardio can be an important part of a training program for some, and unnecessary for others.

If your main goal is to lose fat, cardio in conjunction with weight lifting can be very helpful. To add cardio to your program, your first action step should be to increase your daily activity. This can be done with formal cardio exercises (20 to 30 minutes on a treadmill, elliptical, Airdyne, etc.) or by taking a few 10-minute walks throughout the day. Luckily, technology has made it easier than ever to track our activity, whether it's the Health app on an iPhone, or a fitness tracker like the FitBit or Apple Watch.

On the other hand, cardio is less important if your goal is to build muscle. You will get most, if not all, the cardiovascular health benefits you need just from lifting weights.

WEIGHT LIFTING AND NUTRITION

A well-balanced diet with lots of fruits, vegetables, and plenty of water is always a good idea, and it will only help your progress as you develop a weight lifting program. The nutrition information you need as you begin your weight lifting program is focused on nourishing your body, rather than counting calories.

PROTEIN (20G)	CARBOHYDRATES (30G)	FAT (15G)
3 whole eggs (also counts as a fat serving)	½ cup oatmeal	2 tablespoons peanut butter
5 egg whites	⅔ cup rice	1 ounce almonds
3 ounces chicken breast	3 to 4 rice cakes	1 ounce walnuts
3 ounces whitefish	6 ounces potatoes	1 ounce cashews
3 ounces salmon (also counts as a fat serving)	1 medium apple	1 ounce seeds (such as pumpkin or sunflower)
3 ounces lean red meat (may count as a fat depending on the cut)	1 medium orange	¾ whole avocado
3 ounces turkey	2 cups berries	4 ounces olives
3 ounces lean pork	1 medium banana	1 tablespoon olive oil
1 cup low-fat Greek yogurt	2 cups carrots	3 egg yolks
1 cup low-fat cottage cheese	Broccoli	6 ounces salmon
2½ cups low-fat milk	Cucumbers	40 grams (1.4 ounces) dark chocolate
6 ounces tofu	Mixed salad greens	2 cups full-fat dairy

Protein is, arguably, the most important nutrient you need to build and maintain muscle. I recommend having at least one serving with each meal. When possible, choose lean meats and low-fat dairy options.

Another important nutrient is fat, but select good fats your body requires to function, such as omega-3 acids, which are found in foods such as salmon, leafy green vegetables, and nuts. Whenever possible, avoid high-fat processed foods and fried foods.

"Carbohydrate" became a dirty word somewhere along the way, but a diet full of quality carbs is important for a healthy way of life. Fruits and vegetables are never a bad choice. They provide a range of important nutrients and vitamins your body needs.

To get the most out of your workouts, it's important to consume a pre- and post-workout meal or snack, about 30 to 90 minutes before and after the workout. I recommend a mix of protein, carbohydrates, and fat for each. Make healthy snacks by combining items across the categories on the previous page.

For example: a banana with a couple tablespoons of peanut butter and a glass of low-fat milk; a cup of low-fat Greek yogurt with berries and an ounce of your favorite nuts; scrambled eggs with 3 ounces of turkey and some mixed greens; or rice cakes topped with tuna and avocado will give you an energy boost to sustain you through your workout. Of course, you might simply want to snack on a piece of fruit by itself, or a handful of nuts, which will do the trick and are easy to take with you when you're on the go—just remember to always stay hydrated!

CHAPTER 2

WHERE TO LIFT AND WHAT YOU'LL NEED

The two questions to answer before getting started on your strength training journey are: Where are you going to weight lift? and, What will you need? There are a few different answers. You can buy equipment and work out at home, go the traditional gym route, or look into a private training option. What you choose will depend on your personal preferences, your location, and your budget. This chapter will walk you through all of your options when it comes to the where and the what, and will present the pros and the cons of each to help you pick the right fit.

WHERE TO LIFT WEIGHTS

Whether you choose to work out at home or in a commercial gym facility, most exercises in this book can be done at either place.

At Home

When I was in high school, I had a home gym in my parents' garage. I loved having equipment at the house. It was especially convenient when I couldn't get a ride to the gym! Training at home is a great option if you are busy and short on time. While working out in the comfort of your own home helps eliminate a lot of potential excuses, there are some potential downsides.

The number one issue with creating a home gym is cost. You can start slowly and build your home gym over time, but the up-front investment may be pricy. It's not uncommon to spend $500 on the low end for equipment, or up to a few thousand dollars for more bells and whistles. If you feel comfortable enough with gym equipment that you know what to look for, consider buying used before heading to your local sporting goods store for new.

People are always getting rid of old exercise equipment on Facebook Marketplace, Craigslist, yard sales, etc.

Another downside to consider is the possibility of too many interruptions. It can be hard to focus on your workouts while your kids are running around, or with a television nearby. Find a dedicated workout location at home—away from distractions—and let everyone know the time you plan to lift. Garages or basements tend to be the best spots, but a spare bedroom, or even the living room with the coffee table pushed out of the way, will work if that's what you have available. One thing to keep in mind, wherever you work out, is flooring. It's a good idea to put down some rubber flooring or removable mats not only to protect your equipment but also your home's floors.

Finally, safety can be a concern. If you are training at home by yourself without a spotter, always stop a couple reps short of failure. It's also a good idea to lift weights while someone else is home, just in case of emergency.

Once you have the space ready to go, it's time to get equipment in place. This is the basic equipment I think is necessary to start a home gym. You'll find more detail about it a bit later in this chapter (page 20).

I recommend starting with a **squat rack** or a **squat stand**. This is the cornerstone of the home gym. It allows you to do many different exercises all in one place. It's likely to be the largest expense, but you get what you pay for. A well-made squat rack or squat stand will last a long time.

The next piece of equipment I recommend is a **barbell**. Most barbells come packaged in a 300-pound set, which should be more than enough to get you started. After that I recommend an **adjustable bench**. Finally, invest in a few **dumbbells** and **resistance bands** to round out your home gym. This basic setup should take you a long way in your weight lifting journey.

Of course, you can always add to your collection. Kettlebells, a pull-up bar, a dip bar, and cardio equipment are all nice accessories.

At the Gym

Although training at home has many advantages, by far the most popular place to train is at a standard commercial gym. Besides the huge assortment of equipment available there, you will also be surrounded by like-minded individuals who can provide inspiration or instruction.

Gym Etiquette 101

1. **Use a towel and wipe down all equipment:** This seems like common sense but, believe me, it's not. When you get all sweaty and gross, be courteous to others and wipe down the equipment when you're done. Most gyms have sanitized wipes available near all machines for just this purpose.

2. **Put away all your equipment:** This is the biggest pet peeve of every gym employee. When you use dumbbells, barbells, weight plates, etc., put them back where they belong. Don't leave them on the gym floor; don't leave plates on barbells and machines. These issues prevent people from using equipment and can be dangerous.

3. **Step away from the dumbbell rack:** It's common for people to grab a set of dumbbells and stand right next to the rack. This blocks everyone else from being able to grab their own dumbbells to use.

4. **Give people some space:** Be aware of your surroundings. Give people plenty of room to move. You don't want to accidentally get hit by a free weight! And try to refrain from unnecessary conversation— nothing is worse than losing count of your reps because someone wants to chat.

5. **Don't block anyone's view of the mirror:** The mirror is sacred at the gym. Everyone wants to be able to see their form and catch a glimpse of their physique in action.

6. **Always assume equipment is in use:** If it looks like a piece of equipment is in use, assume it is. Find out if anyone in the area is using the equipment in question, and if they are, simply ask if they would mind if you "work in," which just means share.

There can be a lot of anxiety around going to a big gym when first starting out. No one wants to feel self-conscious, judged, or like they don't belong. The best way to overcome this kind of stress is through experience, but that doesn't help you get your foot in the door.

If you are feeling anxious about going to the gym, here are a few things you can do to ease the stress.

BRING A FRIEND: Bringing a workout friend to the gym is one of the best ways to overcome gym anxiety. With a friend you might feel more comfortable and relaxed—and you'll have more fun.

PLAN YOUR WORKOUT AHEAD OF TIME: If you know exactly what you are going to do, you can eliminate the awkwardness of wandering around looking for available equipment.

GO TO THE GYM WHEN IT IS LESS CROWDED: I have been going to the gym for 15 years and a crowded gym still gives me anxiety! Ask the staff what times are nonpeak hours and plan to go then, if possible, or at least until you feel more comfortable. Most gyms offer a free week (or at least a free day) before you join so you can check it out for yourself.

Here are a few things to look for when choosing a gym:

ATMOSPHERE: Gym atmosphere is really important. Odds are, you won't want to regularly go somewhere dark and dingy. When you walk in, make sure the staff is there to greet you and answer any questions.

LOCATION: When gym shopping, try to find a gym close to home or your work. Over the years I have found my clients are more likely to make it to the gym consistently if it's easy to get to.

PRICE: A commercial gym will typically charge between $30 and 60 per month, with a discount for a longer commitment.

EQUIPMENT: Make sure the gym has the equipment you need, and that it is in good working condition. Be wary of lots of "out of order" signs. It's also nice if the gym has multiple pieces of the main equipment to avoid the frustration of waiting in line to use something. Your gym should have, at least, the following equipment:

> **BARBELLS/DUMBBELLS:** All gyms have barbells and dumbbells, but it's important to check their condition. Are the barbells bent and rusty, or new and shiny? Are the dumbbells bent and falling apart, or in good condition?

CABLE/PULLEY MACHINE: A cable/pulley machine is like the squat rack of machines. You can do many different exercises on it, such as rows, curls, pressdowns, pulldowns, flys, and more.

LAT PULLDOWN: The lat pulldown is one of the most popular pieces of equipment in any gym. In addition to lat pulldowns, you can do triceps pressdowns, facepulls, and a number of other movements on them.

OPEN SPACE: In addition to equipment, make sure your gym has open space to do lunges, warm-ups, stretching, etc.

SQUAT RACK: You can do almost anything in a squat rack. It's the most versatile piece of equipment in the gym. Make sure the gym you choose has more than one.

With a Private Trainer

If you desire more one-on-one attention, working with a trainer in person or online can be a great way to get individualized instruction. The online personal training industry has grown rapidly in recent years because it's a way to reap the benefits of an in-person trainer at a fraction of the cost—though they won't be as hands-on about correcting your form.

Semi-private group training has gained a lot of traction in recent years as well. From a social standpoint, it can't be beat! Plus, training with others can push you a little harder than training alone, and it provides accountability partners to help keep you motivated. Group training is also a more affordable way to work with a personal trainer, though it will still be more expensive than a regular gym membership. If you're interested in the possibility, ask the staff to set you up with a trainer consultation. Most of the time, the training takes place in the gym. Many gyms even offer free personal training sessions or discounts to new gym members.

Although these are all great options, I want to stress that you can successfully reach your goals without a personal trainer. I recommend starting on your own and using a trainer as a backup, should you need more help.

MUST-HAVES AND NICE-TO-HAVES

The good thing about weight lifting is you don't need much equipment to start. Below, I'll go into detail about things I feel are essential to your success and those that are helpful, but not strictly necessary.

Must-Haves

I think you can have everything you need with just five pieces of gym equipment, but equipment isn't the only thing to think about when starting your journey.

ADJUSTABLE BENCH: An adjustable bench can be used for barbell bench presses, dumbbell bench presses, dumbbell rows, chest-supported dumbbell rows, bench dips, core movements, and more.

BARBELLS: When you think of lifting weights, the first thing you probably think of is a barbell. This instrument is critical for all the old-school exercises such as squats, bench presses, deadlifts, rows, and curls.

DUMBBELLS: Similar to barbells, the options with this piece of equipment are just as varied. Dumbbells are great for working one arm or one leg at a time.

RESISTANCE BANDS: From a value standpoint these are fantastic. They are inexpensive, don't take up much room, and can be used for various exercises. The great thing about resistance bands is that, unlike barbells or dumbbells, they offer constant tension.

SQUAT RACK/SQUAT STAND: As mentioned already, this is the most important piece of equipment in any gym, and an important starting point for a home gym. The exercise options using it are nearly endless.

Although free weights (barbells and dumbells), are generally considered to be the most effective exercise equipment, that doesn't mean weight lifting machines and equipment don't have a place in a well-constructed program.

How to Select the Right Weights

For beginners, one of the most important things to understand is how much weight to use. There is no "right" amount of weight—you will determine what is right for you as you begin your program. Because your immediate goal is learning proper technique, you should use weights that are somewhat light and easy to lift. If you start with too much weight, you will use muscles you shouldn't be working and you won't learn good form. As you progress, increase the amount of weight lifted so your muscles adapt and get stronger.

Practice the exercises until you know how to perform them correctly, and then challenge yourself to do sufficient sets to take you close to muscle failure—the point where you can barely get through that last rep. You want to stop *before* you reach complete muscle failure, so stop when you think you can do only one to three more reps.

Remember: If your form breaks down during the set, the weight was too heavy and, if you don't feel challenged at the end, it was too light. Keep adjusting your weights until you find the amount that works for you as a beginner.

The biggest difference between free weights and machines is that machines are fixed in place and only move in certain (typically linear) directions. Due to this fixed nature, there isn't much of a learning curve to perform the movement correctly. On the other hand, free weights can be moved in any direction. Free weights also force you to use more stabilizer muscles to control the weight. Because of this, they require a little more technique.

Another thing to consider is what you'll actually wear while you work out. Having workout gear that is comfortable to move around in and breathable is essential—and if it makes you feel confident and strong when you wear it, even better! But the most important part of your weight lifting gym outfit is footwear. You want a shoe that is comfortable, but that is also compatible with weight training. A typical running shoe is not the best option, nor is a basketball shoe. For lifting weights, you want a shoe with a relatively hard, flat sole without much give. Look for a specified training shoe, or even Converse Chuck Taylors or Vans. Keep in mind that these shoes are for lifting weights, not running.

Nice-to-Haves

The list of nice-to-haves is almost endless, ranging from a basic kettlebell to the most intricate exercise equipment available. Here are a few optional items that can come in handy if your budget allows.

FOAM ROLLERS: A foam roller helps alleviate muscle knots and stimulates blood flow to enhance performance and the recovery process. The rollers are used to apply sustained pressure on connective tissue called myofascia. This technique is considered "self-myofascial release." It offers an effective and affordable way to achieve a similar feel and response provided by a deep-tissue massage.

KETTLEBELLS: Kettlebells have become more popular over the 10 years since I started in the fitness industry. Then, it was rare to see a kettlebell in a gym; now, it's rare if a gym doesn't have any. You can do many different movements with this, but the kettlebell swing is probably the most versatile for building total-body strength, power, and balance, while also improving cardiovascular stamina.

PULL-UP/DIP STATION: Although they are technically bodyweight exercises, pull-ups and dips are some of the most effective movements to build muscle and strength.

CHAPTER 3

SAFETY FIRST

This is, arguably, the most important chapter in the book. It is hard to make progress if you are injured and need to take time away from lifting. This chapter dives deeper into issues mentioned previously, such as the importance of warming up and cooling down, and describes other ways you can prevent injury.

WARMING UP

Whether you are excited to start lifting or just short on time, skipping your warm-up is not the best way to begin a workout. Warm muscles are less likely to become injured and they perform better, helping you get the most out of your gym time.

There are two types of warm-up exercises: **general** and **specific**.

GENERAL WARM-UP: The purpose of the general warm-up is to increase your core temperature and warm up the whole body. Five minutes jumping rope, walking on a treadmill, or using an exercise bike is enough time to get a little sweat going.

SPECIFIC WARM-UP: This activity moves the body through a similar range of motion to what you will do during the workout. There will be more information on the muscle-specific warm-ups in the next section.

BREATHING

Breathing is an important tenet of weight lifting. For most exercises, you inhale on the way down and exhale on the way up—and never hold your breath during the movement.

That said, some exercises—specifically compound exercises—make it nearly impossible to breathe during the rep and, at times, holding your breath is the right way to go. Inhaling and holding your breath on exertion can help provide greater muscular force and more core stability, which helps prevent lower back injuries. If you picked up the end of your couch, you would automatically hold your breath and breathe again once it was lifted. This is what you should do when lifting heavy weights (when you are ready).

PROPER FORM

Learning proper form is critical to being successful in weight lifting. The right technique allows you to engage the correct muscles and prevent injury in the most effective manner. Pay attention to which muscles you feel working during the exercise. If it is not the intended muscle group, that usually means your form is off.

These tips will help you practice proper form:

START LIGHT: Lifting too much weight is the biggest reason people have sloppy form. When you are just beginning, use a light weight and go heavier only when your technique is rock solid. It's much easier to use good form with a weight light enough to control.

RECORD A VIDEO OF YOURSELF: The way an exercise feels as you do it might not be the same way it looks. Record a video of yourself performing your set and compare it to the examples in the book to make sure your form is correct. You can also do your routine in front of a full-length mirror to get a visual of your form.

COOLING DOWN

At the end of each exercise session, cool down for a few minutes. This is the best time to work on flexibility. While lifting weights, you contract, or shorten, your muscles, causing them to become tight. Stretching loosens the muscles and increases their range of motion. Light stretches help bring your heart rate down and give you time to mentally prepare for the rest of your day.

During your cooldown, focus on static stretching, likely the style of stretching you did in gym class growing up. An example is the classic sit and reach, where you lean forward and touch your toes. There is more information on specific stretches to do during cooldown for each muscle group in the next section.

REST AND RECOVERY

The amount of time needed for your muscles to recover between workouts is influenced by many factors, including how much exercise was done, how intense the exercise was, your sleep habits, nutrition, training experience, and, most importantly, genetics. When you're first starting, your body isn't accustomed to lifting weights and engaging those muscles. For this reason, I recommend longer recovery periods between workouts. As mentioned earlier, the time out of the gym is when actual progress is made, so it's important to stay within your body's ability to recover from your workouts.

Try to give each muscle group 48 to 72 hours of recovery time between workouts. This is best accomplished through full-body training every other day, for a maximum of three days per week.

Common Weight Lifting Injuries and How to Avoid Them

Here are the most common injury complaints I hear from new lifters, and ways to prevent or treat them.

Lower back pain: The best way to avoid one of the most common injuries is always to use good form when weight lifting. One thing to keep in mind with lower back pain is the complexity with which this injury can occur. Pain that shows up in the lower back may be due to tight hips from sitting all day, ankle immobility, or a number of other things. The good news is, most lower back pain improves after a few days of rest. If the pain doesn't subside after four to five days, see a doctor.

Shoulder pain: The shoulder joint is very susceptible to injury, in part because it's made up of a bunch of small muscles and also due to the nature of a ball-and-socket joint. One of the easiest ways to keep your shoulders healthy is to include a lot of horizontal rowing exercises in your program. Doing too many pressing movements, such as a bench press, without enough rowing movements, like a dumbbell row, can lead to bad posture, muscle tightness, and muscular imbalances. To keep shoulders healthy, do an equal number of rowing and pressing exercises, or even twice as many rowing as pressing exercises.

If you feel shoulder pain, identify the movement causing the pain, remove the exercise from your routine, and look for a replacement. Remember: There is no exercise you *have* to do. There is always another option.

Sore knees: Knee pain is most often caused by a form breakdown during lower-body exercises. If you feel knee pain, take a look at your knee positioning during squats. Don't allow your knees to turn in toward each other during the movement. If you do experience knee pain, it is most likely inflammation that can be mitigated by ice and/or NSAIDs, if you tolerate them.

FREE WEIGHT SAFETY

The free weight section of the gym is, by far, the most intimidating for beginners. Aside from the normal anxiety caused just by going to the gym, a general fear of injury is common when using free weights if you don't have a solid foundation for proper use. Here are a few tips to help you navigate the free weight area of the gym safely.

ALWAYS USE COLLARS ON BARBELL EXERCISES: A "collar" or "clip" is used at the end of the barbell to secure the weights and prevent them from falling off during the exercise.

HAVE A SPOTTER, WHEN NECESSARY: A spotter is there to help you. Any exercise for which you can't set the weights down safely on your own requires a spotter. A good example is the bench press. If you are not working out with a friend, ask one of the gym employees or gym members to spot you.

PAY ATTENTION TO LOADING AND UNLOADING WEIGHTS: Free weight safety isn't limited only to the exercises themselves. When you are in the gym, always pay attention to your surroundings. One of my clients broke his toe unloading a weight plate off a barbell, not realizing there were actually two weight plates on the bar, causing the second one to fall on his toe. Ouch!

PICK THE RIGHT SIZE WEIGHT: Weight selection can be tricky to navigate, especially at first. How much weight you use will depend on your strength level. Start light and pick a heavier weight only if you can complete all your reps with perfect form. Keep good notes on how heavy the weight felt, how many reps you did, and for how many sets. Use this information to help you select the correct weight the following week.

WEIGHT MACHINE SAFETY

Although weight machines are generally considered safer than free weights, there are still a few things to watch out for, especially as a beginner:

CUSTOM FIT EACH MACHINE: Most gym machines have multiple adjustments to account for every body type. Take advantage of this. The better the machine fits your specific dimensions, the more effective it will be. If the machine is not properly adjusted, it can cause injury.

DON'T REINVENT THE WHEEL: It's common for people to get creative with exercise machines and try to invent new ways to use them. This is not a good idea. Use the machine the way it is intended to be used.

STAY IN CONTROL: As the machine is in a fixed plane and doesn't require any stabilization, it's common for people to increase their speed when performing an exercise. This can lead to a lack of control. Always use a slow and controlled rep cadence; this is not only the most effective way to lift weights, it also is the safest.

WATCH YOUR HANDS AND FINGERS: *Keep all hands and feet inside the machine at all times*. Although that sounds like a sign at an amusement park, it's very important for machine training. Be mindful of where the weight stack is located, where all the moving parts are, etc.

PART TWO

BASIC EXERCISES FOR BEGINNERS

THIS SECTION breaks down the fundamental exercises in easy-to-follow steps so you'll know exactly what to do in your workouts.

Carefully study the instructions for each exercise before beginning to ensure you do it safely and get the most out of each exercise. Details matter, and it's easiest to learn them correctly from the beginning. Along with the specifics of form, pay attention to issues such as foot placement and grip.

Remember, everyone has unique limb lengths and biomechanics. Proper form may look a little different for you versus your workout partner. Use the information in this section as a solid starting point, and as you gain experience, you will find what works best for you.

LEGS AND GLUTES

Having strong, functional legs is important. Your legs bring you from place to place, so building strength in your lower half, glutes included, is crucial. As you start, focus on the basics before moving on to the more involved and complicated modifications.

With any beginner program, less is more. Don't overload your body with a bunch of exercises (or weight) right off the bat. Make no mistake: Lower body training adds up quickly. The leg muscles and glutes are big muscles that require hard work to be trained effectively. Because of this, lower-body workouts often require more effort per exercise and produce more fatigue than upper-body workouts. Don't let this discourage you. Embrace the challenge and know you'll benefit from taking lower-body training seriously.

This program incorporates a few exercises that train each leg individually. This ensures equal muscle development, which helps improve balance and coordination.

AIR SQUAT

Primary Muscles Involved: Quadriceps, Hamstrings, Glutes

The air squat is the most basic fundamental movement. It not only reinforces the squat movement pattern, but it also gets the lower body warmed up and ready to perform. This is one exercise for which it's okay to do a few extra reps if you need to. Sometimes it may take a little longer to get into a groove where you feel warmed up and ready to move on to a loaded squat variation.

Instructions

1. Start in a standing position with your feet about shoulder-width apart.

2. Drop your hips back like you are sitting in a chair, while simultaneously bending your knees. Continue moving down until your hips are below the tops of your knees.

3. Once you reach the bottom of the position, stand up. To help with balance, extend your arms directly in front of you during the movement.

Dos and Don'ts

✅ When performing the air squat, keep your torso as vertical as possible.

❌ Don't bend forward at the waist during the movement or lean too far forward.

TIP: *When performing the air squat, keep most of your bodyweight on your heels and away from your toes.*

Try This!

BOX AIR SQUAT: If you struggle to reach depth when air squatting, try sitting on a box or bench that requires your knees to be at a 90-degree angle until you feel comfortable doing the squat without it.

PAUSED AIR SQUAT: If you want a harder variation on the air squat, try the paused air squat. When you reach the bottom position, pause for 1 to 2 seconds before returning to standing.

DUMBBELL GOBLET SQUAT

Primary Muscles Involved: Quadriceps, Hamstrings, Glutes

The goblet squat is the perfect introduction to a loaded squat movement pattern. Named for the way in which you hold the weight—in front of your chest, with your hands cupped—the goblet squat teaches you to maintain an upright position while dropping into the squat position.

Instructions:

1. Start in a standing position with your feet about shoulder-width apart, holding a dumbbell against your chest.

2. Drop your hips back like you are sitting in a chair, while simultaneously bending your knees. Continue moving down until your hips are below the tops of your knees.

3. Once you reach the bottom of the position, stand up and return to your starting position. Your upper body should hardly move during the exercise if you're using your legs, hips, and lower back as one unit.

Dos and Don'ts

✓ The biggest thing to remember when performing the goblet squat is to hold the dumbbell tightly against your chest. This helps reinforce the upright positioning we want to keep throughout the entire movement.

✗ Don't allow the weight to pull you forward.

TIP: *When dropping into the squat, push your knees out to the sides while keeping your entire foot on the ground. This helps prevent your knees from caving in during the rep.*

Try This!

BOX GOBLET SQUAT: If you struggle reaching depth, try sitting on a box or bench that requires your knees to be at a 90-degree angle until you feel comfortable doing the squat without it.

BARBELL BACK SQUAT: When you are comfortable with the dumbbell goblet squat, advance to a traditional barbell back squat. The advantage of this is the ability to use more weight. The squat movement pattern is the same, but the barbell is placed on your trapezius muscles, which are in your upper middle back, between or slightly above your shoulder blades.

BARBELL ROMANIAN DEADLIFT

Primary Muscles Involved: Hamstrings, Glutes, Back

The Romanian deadlift (RDL) is the main hip hinge movement for this program. Unlike the traditional deadlift, the RDL focuses more on the hamstrings, and in fact, is one of the best exercises for those muscles. The first time you do this, don't be surprised if your hamstrings are really sore the next day.

Instructions:

1. Start with the barbell in a rack, just above your knees. Stand with your feet about shoulder-width apart.

2. Grab the bar with an overhand grip (both palms facing down) or a mixed grip (one palm facing up, one facing down), brace your core, and lift the bar out of the rack by extending your knees. From there, take a step back to get into starting position.

3. Brace your core once again, and begin the exercise by hinging at the hips. Bend forward and push your hips back as the bar slides down your thighs. Maintain a slight bend in the knees during the movement.

4. Once the bar is lowered to mid-shin, reverse the movement by driving the hips forward and extending the torso back to the starting position.

Dos and Don'ts

✓ Keep the bar close to your body. It should stay in contact with your body the entire time, sliding up and down your legs.

✗ Don't bend your knees too much. Maintain only a slight bend in your knees and keep your hips high throughout the entire movement. If you can't do this without bending your knees too much, you are probably using too much weight.

> **TIP:** *The point of this deadlift is to get a good stretch in your hamstrings. It's not about how much weight you can lift.*

Try This!

DUMBBELL ROMANIAN DEADLIFT: If you can't maintain proper form using a barbell, use dumbbells instead.

SINGLE-LEG DUMBBELL ROMANIAN DEADLIFT: If the barbell RDL is not challenging enough for you, shift to a pair of dumbbells and stand on one foot, allowing the other to extend backward as you do the movement.

DUMBBELL STEP-UP

Primary Muscles Involved: Quadriceps, Hamstrings, Glutes

This exercise is great for developing muscle and strength while also improving balance. You'll need a sturdy box that can hold your weight (or a stable flat surface like a bench) that is 12 to 18 inches (30 to 46 cm) high, or whatever height you need to create a 90-degree angle at the knee joint when your foot is resting on it.

Instructions:

1. Hold the dumbbells at your sides standing about 12 inches (30 cm) away from the box.

2. Step up with one leg to place the entire foot on the box.

3. As you step up on the box, keep your torso erect and avoid leaning forward. Push off with the lead leg, already on the box, and bring your back foot onto the box.

4. Once both feet are on the box, pause for 1 second before returning both feet to the ground, one at a time.

5. Repeat with your other leg.

Dos and Don'ts

✔ Maintain your balance. Pick a spot on the wall and focus on it during the entire set. It sounds strange, but it will help you maintain balance.

✖ The biggest mistake people make is using too much weight, which causes you to lean forward as you step up. This also puts your lower back in a position to become injured. It's important to start with light weights. Once you can do the exercise correctly, add more weight. You might find starting with just your bodyweight is best.

TIP: *If you can't maintain your grip on the dumbbells, there are some accessories that might help you. Lifting chalk dusted onto your hands or the use of lifting straps might make a difference.*

Try This!

BODYWEIGHT STEP-UPS: For beginners, start with just your bodyweight. Do the exercise as indicated, and when you feel more comfortable, add weight.

DUMBBELL LUNGES: If you don't have a box to use, the dumbbell lunge is a great modification. Stand upright with the dumbbells at your sides, palms facing your body. Lunge forward as far as you can with your right leg, bending your left knee so it almost brushes the floor. Return to the starting position and repeat with the opposite leg.

DUMBBELL BULGARIAN SPLIT SQUAT

Primary Muscles Involved: Quadriceps, Hamstrings, Glutes

This is a great squat because it's so safe to do and, if you have a lower back injury, it's a terrific replacement for the back squat. The dumbbell Bulgarian split squat (BSS) is another single-leg exercise that will develop your lower body.

Instructions:

1. Hold one dumbbell at each side while standing with a bench behind you.

2. Reach one leg behind you and rest the top of your foot on the bench.

3. Brace your core and descend, with control, until your back knee is a couple of inches (about 5 cm) from the ground or your front thigh is parallel to the ground.

4. Extend your knees and hips to return to the starting position. Keep your torso upright during the entire rep.

Dos and Don'ts

✔ If the exercise feels awkward, try leaning forward at the waist slightly.

✖ Don't stand too far away or too close to the bench. You'll have to try different distances until you find the right placement, so you can complete the movement with good form. If the bench is too far away, you'll have trouble keeping your torso upright, and you may end up with pain in your hips. If you stand too close to the bench, your knee will have to move too far forward, which is likely to cause knee pain. With trial and error you'll find the perfect spot somewhere in the middle.

TIP: *If you're working out at the gym and there is a lying leg-curl machine, try placing your back foot on the leg pad. Because it rolls, the movement is a little easier to do.*

Try This!

BODYWEIGHT BULGARIAN SPLIT SQUAT: Beginners may find it difficult to do this exercise with good form. If you need to, use only your bodyweight while completing the exercise.

BARBELL BULGARIAN SPLIT SQUAT: If you need a little more challenge, use a barbell instead of the dumbbells. Do the exercise the same way, but with the barbell in the back squat (page 39) position, in the upper middle part of your back.

DUMBBELL LUNGE

Primary Muscles Involved: Quadriceps, Hamstrings, Glutes

The dumbbell lunge is one of the most popular lower-body exercises, and it's one of my all-time favorites. One of the biggest benefits to this movement is that it works on balance as well as muscular strength.

Instructions:

1. Start from a standing position with two dumbbells, one at each side.

2. Take one step forward, about 2 feet or so, and lower your body so your back knee touches the floor. Keep your balance and hold your torso upright.

3. Push up, mostly using the heel of your standing foot, and return to a standing position.

4. Using the same leg, step forward and repeat the movement. When you have completed the desired number of reps, switch legs and do the same number of reps.

Dos and Don'ts

✓ With this exercise, it's important to use a full range of motion. Make sure you touch your back knee to the ground during each rep.

✗ Stepping too far forward will make it hard to maintain your balance. Both legs should be bent at roughly 90 degrees in the bottom position of the movement.

TIP: *Maintain a hip-width stance with each forward step. Avoid bringing your front foot directly in line with your back foot, as if you're walking on a tightrope.*

Try This!

BODYWEIGHT LUNGES:
If weighted lunges are too difficult at first, just use your bodyweight.

BARBELL LUNGES: Instead of dumbbells, use a barbell. The exercise is performed the same way, except with a barbell in the back squat position.

HURDLE STRETCH

Primary Muscles Involved: Quadriceps, Hamstrings, Glutes, Hip

The hurdle stretch is essential to any routine because it stretches tight hip flexors and hamstrings. Though most commonly used as a warm-up exercise, this simple stretch is best done *after* exercise—not before—once your muscles are more receptive to the stretch.

Instructions:

1. Take a seated position on the floor and extend one leg at a 45-degree angle from your hips.

2. Position your other leg straight out in front of you.

3. Reach along the straight leg as far as you can and hold the stretch.

Dos and Don'ts

✓ Try to progress and deepen the stretch a little more each week.

✗ It may be easier to bend your knee, but extend your leg as straight as possible and reach as far as you can.

TIP: *Stretching should not be excruciatingly painful. Only stretch to mild discomfort.*

Try This!

SIT AND REACH: For some people, the hurdle stretch position will be uncomfortable. If it is for you, sit with both legs extended in front of you and stretch forward.

COUCH STRETCH: For a more advanced stretch, try the couch stretch. Begin by getting into the same position as the Dumbbell Bulgarian Split Squat (page 44), except now you want your back knee to touch the ground and your back foot on the couch. The knee should be in a straight line with the front edge of the couch. Initiate the stretch by pressing your hip forward, away from the couch. Repeat on the other side.

BACK

It's very common to neglect back training, which is a mistake! Strong upper-back muscles are important in everyday life. They make it easier to do regular tasks like dragging your suitcases through airport terminals, moving a piece of furniture, or taking your dog for a walk. They're also important for injury prevention. Strong upper-back muscles keep your shoulders healthy; as your lats do most of the work in all the pulling movements, building strength there takes the load off your shoulders. They support your spine and, of course they have an important role in good posture, helping you stand straighter and taller and opening your chest.

There are three important back muscles to know about. Your lats (latissimus dorsi) pull your arms toward your body and run from just behind each armpit to the center of your lower back. If you swim a lot, you probably have strong lats. Your traps (trapezius) stabilize your shoulders and help you shrug, move your head to the back or side, and look behind you. Finally, your rhomboids sit between your spine and shoulder blades. If you sit for long hours at a desk or computer, you probably have weak rhomboids.

As a beginner, back training should be an essential part of your program.

ROPE LAT EXTENSION

Primary Muscles Involved: Latissimus Dorsi (Lats)

This is a great way to warm up your back muscles using equipment at the gym. The rope lat extension is one of the few exercises that focus exclusively on the lats, which means that because you aren't using your biceps, you'll really be able to feel your lats doing the work.

Instructions:

1. Attach a rope to a high cable pulley and stand a couple of feet away from the stack.

2. With your feet at shoulder width, facing the stack, grasp the rope with both hands and lean forward from the hips with your arms extended up in front of you. This is the starting position.

3. Keeping your arms straight, pull the rope down toward your thighs. Your hands should end up next to your hips.

4. From the hips, return the rope to the starting position in a controlled fashion.

Dos and Don'ts

✓ Once you get into the correct position, lock your arms nearly straight and keep them in that position for the duration of the set.

✗ This exercise is not a triceps press-down, even if it looks similar from a distance. Don't change your elbow angle. With elbows straight, you may feel the work in your triceps a little, but the exercise focuses on the lats.

TIP: *The rope attachment should be set higher than head level.*

Try This!

STRAIGHT-BAR LAT EXTENSION:
Instead of using a rope attachment, use a straight bar, which is a little easier because it reduces the range of motion.

SINGLE-ARM ROPE LAT EXTENSION: For a slightly more advanced option, do the single-arm rope lat extension, which is essentially the same movement, just using one arm at a time.

LAT PULLDOWN

Primary Muscles Involved: Latissimus Dorsi (Lats)

Whatever the type of gym you train in, odds are you'll have a lat pulldown machine to use. This accessibility, combined with how easy the exercise is to perform, has made it a staple in many gymgoers' routines. The key for it to be truly effective, however, is to do the exercise correctly, as I outline below.

Instructions:

1. Sit facing the machine with your legs positioned under the pads, gripping the bar with an overhand grip placed wider than shoulder width.

2. Slightly arch your back while pulling the bar down and toward the upper chest.

3. Once the bar comes within 1 to 2 inches of the upper chest, slowly return to the starting position.

Dos and Don'ts

✔ Use a full range of motion. Start with your arms fully locked out and pull down until the bar reaches your upper chest.

✖ Don't lean too far back. Do not turn this into a rowing movement. Aim to maintain as vertical a torso angle as possible while having a slight arch in the back.

TIP: *If you feel your biceps are compensating and you can't "feel it in your back," try a "false grip"—not wrapping your thumb around the bar. Think of your hands as hooks and drive down with your elbows.*

Try This!

GRIP OPTIONS: Although grip variations are not necessarily easier, you may be able to find a grip that is more comfortable for you. Try changing your grip from two-handed to one-handed, from narrow to wide, or from overhand to underhand.

PULL-UP: The pull-up is a more challenging version of the lat pulldown movement pattern. Maintaining a shoulder-width grip, grab the pull-up bar with an overhand grip. Hang with your arms straight and your legs off the floor. Pull yourself up by pulling your elbows down to the floor and continue until your chin passes the bar. Lower yourself until your arms are straight.

HOME WORKOUT HACK: *To do this at home, you can substitute pull-ups if you have a pull-up bar.*

DUMBBELL ROW

Primary Muscles Involved: Latissimus Dorsi (Lats), Teres Major, Rhomboids

All you need is a dumbbell and a bench for this one. The dumbbell row is a great all-around exercise to build upper-back and lat strength, while giving your lower back a break. Because you work one side at a time, bracing your upper body with one hand, you don't put a lot of pressure on your lower back.

Instructions:

1. Grab a dumbbell with your palm facing in toward your body. Place your opposite hand and knee on a bench or chair for support.

2. Keeping your back straight, pull the dumbbell up and back toward your hip, trying to get the dumbbell as high as possible.

3. At the top of the movement, allow your shoulder blades to move and retract to get the full range of motion.

4. Repeat on the other side.

Dos and Don'ts

✓ Keep your shoulders and torso square during the entire movement. Only the arm and shoulder blade should be moving during the rep.

✗ Too often, people twist their torso in the mistaken belief they are going through a full range of motion. Too much torso rotation limits the activation of your lats.

TIP: *Be sure to use a weight you can handle and do the movements with control. If you use too much weight, you'll accidentally wind up using every muscle except your back.*

Try This!

SINGLE-ARM SEATED CABLE ROW: To maintain the unilateral nature of the movement, the single-arm cable row is a great variation for dumbbell rows.

HAMMER STRENGTH MACHINE ISO ROW: If your gym has this machine, it will give you a fantastic single-arm rowing option.

HOME WORKOUT HACK: *If you have a dumbbell, you can do rows with a chair as support instead of a bench.*

SEATED CABLE ROW

Primary Muscles Involved: Latissimus Dorsi (Lats), Teres Major, Rhomboids

Weight lifters from each end of the experience spectrum love the seated cable row due to its versatility. It can be part of a beginner's routine as easily as it can be part of a more advanced regimen. The machine is available in most gyms and allows you to experiment with multiple grips to find what's most comfortable for you.

Instructions:

1. Sit facing the machine with your feet resting on the foot pad.

2. Grasp the handles with an overhand or neutral grip, depending on the handle selected.

3. Sit in an upright position, with your torso perpendicular to the floor, your knees slightly bent, and your arms extended directly out in front of you. This is the starting position.

4. Begin the movement by pulling the handle toward your abdomen. Once the handle reaches your abdomen, return to the starting position.

Dos and Don'ts

✓ Pull the cable attachment toward your waist and when you get to the full range of motion, hold the position for 1 second before returning to the start. This ensures you use your back to move the weight, and not momentum.

✗ Don't round your back. This exercise maintains a neutral spine. Some people have the mistaken belief that rounding your back when you return to the starting position gives you a longer range of motion. This is not true.

TIP: *To change the angle of the pull, and therefore muscle activation, elevate where you sit by placing a dumbbell or box on the seat pad.*

Try This!

WIDE-GRIP SEATED CABLE ROW: Similar to the Lat Pulldown (page 54), there are a lot of different bars and grips you can use. Try experimenting with a wide grip, a close grip, an underhand grip, a neutral grip (palms facing each other), etc. You may find one grip easier than the others.

SINGLE-ARM SEATED CABLE ROW: The single-arm variation is an excellent exercise to throw in occasionally because it works each side of the back individually.

INVERTED ROW

Primary Muscles Involved: Latissimus Dorsi (Lats), Teres Major, Rhomboids

Inverted rows are one of the most underrated exercises to build upper-back strength. They offer a unique alternative to traditional machine, cable, barbell, and dumbbell rows. Also, if you have lower back pain, inverted rows are a great way to perform a rowing movement while taking most of the pressure off the lower back.

Instructions:

1. Position a bar in a squat rack to about waist height. You can also use a Smith machine, if one is available.

2. Take a wider-than-shoulder-width grip on the bar and position yourself lying down underneath it. Your upper and lower body should both be straight with your heels on the ground and your arms fully extended. This is your starting position.

3. Begin by flexing your elbow and pulling your chest toward the bar. Retract your shoulder blades as you perform the movement. Pause at the top of the motion, and return yourself to the start position.

4. Repeat for the desired number of repetitions.

Dos and Don'ts

✔ Use a full range of motion. This exercise gets harder the closer your chest gets to the bar. Make sure you go all the way up and all the way down to get the most out of the exercise. Keep your body straight during the movement.

✘ Don't let your hips sag.

Try This!

CHEST-SUPPORTED ROW:
A chest-supported row machine offers a great alternative and puts less stress on your lower back. Raise the bench to a 45-degree angle and position your body so your chest is on the inclined bench and you're standing on the balls of your feet. With a dumbbell in each hand and palms facing each other, squeeze your shoulder blades together and bring your elbows toward the ceiling until the dumbbells reach your rib cage. With control, lower the dumbbells to the ground. Repeat for desired number of reps.

FEET-ELEVATED INVERTED ROW: If you want more resistance, elevate your feet on a bench to make the movement more difficult.

HOME WORKOUT HACK: *If you have a very sturdy table, position yourself on the floor underneath it with your legs extended. Grip the tabletop, and pull yourself up. Or tie a knot at one end of a bedsheet, throw it over a door, and close the door tightly so the knot is positioned behind it. Spread out the sheet, grab it with your hands at chest height, and lean back until your arms are straight. Keep your body straight, and drive your elbows back, and then pull forward until your chest reaches your hands. Return to the starting position and repeat.*

BACK EXTENSION

Primary Muscles Involved: Lower Back

Lower-back pain can potentially affect daily activities you might not even think about—from pain when picking up your children to difficulty sleeping. This exercise isolates the muscles of your lower back and allows you to work them safely. Use just your bodyweight to start and add weight as you progress.

Instructions:

1. Lie facedown on a back extension bench. Place your ankles under the roller pads, with your hips resting on the support pad. This is the starting position.

2. With your body straight, cross your arms in front of you and lower your torso forward toward the ground. Once you reach the point where going any further would cause you to arch your back, reverse the movement to return to the starting position.

Dos and Don'ts

✔ Do this exercise slowly and maintain control. It's always a good idea to be extra cautious with the lower back. Your neck should be in line with your spine; don't arch your neck backward.

✖ Don't move farther than a neutral position with your spine. Going into hyperextension at the top of the movement, beyond your spine's neutral position, puts strain on your lower back and doesn't provide any extra training for your muscles.

TIP: *You can cross your arms in front of you on your chest, put them behind your head, or keep them down by your sides. Pick the position that's the most comfortable for you.*

Try This!

KETTLEBELL SWING: Hold a kettlebell between your legs using a two-handed overhand grip and stand with your feet shoulder-width apart and your knees slightly bent. With a slight arch in your lower back, move your hips back until the kettlebell has swung between and behind your legs. Then squeeze your glutes and drive your hips forward to swing the kettlebell up to shoulder height. Let it swing back between your legs and bend your knees slightly as you drive your hips back.

REVERSE HYPER MACHINE: If your gym has a reverse hyper machine, try this exercise to strengthen both your lower back and hamstrings. Put your feet in the straps and place your chest flat on the top pad with your hips hanging off the back of the machine. Grab the handles and drive your legs up toward the ceiling by flexing your hips, glutes, and hamstrings. Keep your legs straight throughout the movement. When your legs are as high as possible, reverse the movement.

HOME WORKOUT HACK: *Lie facedown on the floor with your arms out in front of you and lift your upper body off the ground, bending at the waist, while keeping your lower body and legs on the floor. Raise up a few inches and lower to the starting position to repeat. Be sure to keep your neck in line with your spine and do not arch it.*

LAT STRETCH

Primary Muscles Involved: Back

This simple and easy stretch becomes even more effective with the addition of a foam roller. Exercising your lats can leave them feeling tight and bunched up and lead to things such as shoulder pain, bad posture, and the inability to reach above your head. To avoid discomfort, I suggest doing this lat stretch after every upper-body workout.

Instructions:

1. Stand facing a fixed bar or sturdy support.

2. Grab the bar or support with both hands at about waist height.

3. Allow your hips to fall back while you bend forward. Lean your torso toward the bar/support. Hold the stretch.

Dos and Don'ts

✔ Relax! A mistake people often make with all stretching, not just this lat stretch, is maintaining too much tension in the muscle. Make sure you relax the lats and allow them to actually stretch.

✘ Think of your hands as hooks to attach to the support. The stretch is for your back, not your arms, so don't pull with them.

TIP: *Move your hips from side to side to create a greater stretch in the muscle.*

Try This!

KNEELING LAT STRETCH: This is a good alternative if you need to begin with a slightly easier option. Kneel and hold your hands together while reaching out on the floor in front of you and lowering your shoulder blades toward the ground.

FOAM ROLLING LATS: One of my favorite areas to perform soft tissue work is the lats. Lie on your side with a foam roller tucked underneath your armpits. Apply pressure and slowly roll from your armpits to your lower lats. Spend more time on areas that need it.

ABS AND CORE

Abs and core training has benefits far beyond the coveted six-pack, although many are inspired to work those muscles for that reason alone. Your core protects your internal organs and connects your upper and lower body—it's your entire support system! Anything you do that involves lifting, reaching, twisting, or moving your legs involves those core and ab muscles. Even sitting up straight at your desk or tying your shoes engages your core. A strong core is important for athletic activities, for balance and overall stability, and for simply going about your everyday life. If you've ever had lower back pain, you know how debilitating it can be, and how it affects everything you need or want to do. A strong core plays a part in avoiding lower back injuries, too.

Abs and core muscles are just like every other muscle in your body: They need to be challenged in a consistent way so they can adapt and become stronger. Warm-ups and cooldowns aren't necessary with these muscle groups because they are activated during other exercises.

PLANK

Primary Muscles Involved: Abdominals

Performed correctly, the plank is one of the safest abdominal exercises for your routine. It's an isometric exercise, which means you don't move your joints or muscles, but instead hold the position for a length of time. Because you aren't moving, you might think it's going to be easy or ineffective. Don't be fooled— it's a lot harder than it looks. In addition to building core strength, the plank also helps prevent back pain.

Instructions:

1. Lie facedown on the floor, then lift yourself up using your toes and fore-arms. Your arms should be bent at 90 degrees with your elbows directly under your shoulders and your wrists aligned with your elbows.

2. Once in position, brace your core hard, like you are preparing to get punched in the stomach. Flex your glutes and thigh muscles as well, while continu-ing to breathe normally.

3. Keep your body straight at all times and hold this position for the duration of the set.

Dos and Don'ts

✓ Flex your abs as hard as you can while holding the plank. This helps maintain good position.

✗ Proper form for the plank means keeping your body in a straight line, so don't let your hips sag (or raise) when you are tired.

TIP: *It's easy to forget to breathe when you're doing the plank—but don't hold your breath. If you focus on breathing normally, at regular intervals, it will help distract you from the amount of time remaining in the hold.*

Try This!

KNEE PLANK: To make the plank easier while you're building core strength, do the movement from your knees instead of your toes.

FEET-ELEVATED ONE-LEG PLANK: When you're ready for a challenge, place your feet on an elevated surface. For an even greater challenge, lift one leg slightly off the floor and keep it there for the duration of the hold.

WEIGHTED DECLINE SIT-UP

Primary Muscles Involved: Abdominals

Sometimes people make the mistake of thinking the way to challenge their abs is to do a ton of reps of an easy exercise, but the muscles actually require periods of high resistance to gain strength. Your muscles need to be consistently challenged so they can adapt, and the weighted decline sit-up is a great way to make the standard sit-up more difficult. The addition of gravity and weight resistance will have you working up a sweat in no time. You'll start with a light weight of about 10 pounds and build from there.

Instructions:

1. Secure your legs at the end of the decline bench and lie down. Cross your hands over your chest holding a weight plate. This is the starting position.

2. To begin the movement, push your lower back down into the bench to better isolate your abdominal muscles and begin to roll your shoulders off the bench.

3. Continue sitting up until your arms come in contact with your knees. Hold the top position for 1 second.

4. After the 1-second hold, slowly come down to the starting position.

Dos and Don'ts

✔ This is a decline sit-up, not a decline crunch. Use the full range of motion going all the way down and all the way up.

✘ Don't just use momentum. To get the most out of this exercise, return to the starting position in a controlled fashion. Your core should be tight throughout the entire rep.

TIP: *Make sure you hold the weight close to your chest; don't let it slide down toward your waist.*

Try This!

SIT-UP: You may need to begin with regular sit-ups, if decline sit-ups are too difficult at the start. When sit-ups become less challenging, move to decline sit-ups and, eventually, add a weight for a weighted decline sit-up.

USE A HIGHER DECLINE OR MORE WEIGHT: To make the weighted decline sit-up more difficult, increase the degree of decline or hold a heavier weight.

HOME WORKOUT HACK: *At home do regular sit-ups holding a weight or even a heavy book. Put those old college textbooks to use!*

ROPE CABLE CRUNCH

Primary Muscles Involved: Abdominals

This is a classic upper-abdominal builder. Rope cable crunches can be a little tricky to master at first. The key to making sure your form is correct is to avoid rocking the torso up and down with each rep. Don't get discouraged if you don't feel like you're making progress right away. Once you get the hang of them, rope cable crunches will be a game changer for your ab workouts!

Instructions:

1. Kneel below a high pulley that contains a rope attachment.

2. Grasp both ends of the rope. Pull it down so your hands holding the rope are by your face.

3. Flex your hips slightly and allow the weight to stretch out your lower back. This is your starting position.

4. With your hips fixed, bend your waist as you contract the abs in a crunch motion. Your elbows should move toward the middle of your thighs. Make sure to maintain constant abdominal tension.

5. Hold the contraction for 1 second, keeping constant tension on the abs throughout the movement. After holding the contraction, slowly return to the starting position.

Dos and Don'ts

✓ Put a mat under your knees to make them more comfortable.

✗ The biggest issue with this exercise is using too much weight, which causes you to move the weight stack with muscles other than your abs.

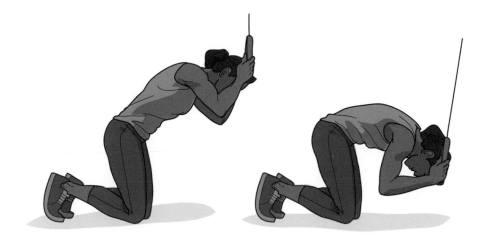

TIP: *You can do this exercise kneeling or standing. Experiment with both versions and select the variation that works best for you.*

Try This!

CRUNCH: Although the crunch is about as basic as it gets, it's still an effective ab exercise you can do anywhere—and is a great home hack. It's an easier variation you can start with to build strength before moving to the cable crunch.

MACHINE CRUNCH: If your gym has the equipment, the machine crunch is a great alternative to the rope cable crunch, and it typically allows you to use more weight/resistance. The key to focus on here is using your abs, not your arms, to move the weight. When you're sitting on the machine, place your feet under the pads and grab the top handles. Contract your abdominals and crunch your upper torso toward your legs.

BICYCLE CRUNCH

Primary Muscles Involved: Abdominals (Obliques)

In the United Kingdom, the United Council on Exercise set out to find the most effective exercise for your abs, and out of 13 go-to exercises, bicycle crunches were voted number one. They target your entire core, including your upper- and lower-abdominals and your obliques—all with one movement. Going slowly and focusing on good form will ensure you get the most out of each rep.

Instructions:

1. Lie flat on the floor with your lower back pressed into the ground. Put your hands behind your head with your elbows flared out to the sides. Your knees should be bent at 90 degrees with your feet flat on the floor. This is your starting position.

2. Lift your shoulders into the crunch position while simultaneously using a bicycle pedal motion to kick forward with the right leg and retract the left knee. Bring your right elbow close to your left knee by crunching to the side. Remember: This isn't about speed; it's about slow, proper form.

3. Return to the starting position.

4. Crunch to the opposite side as you cycle your legs and, this time, lift your left elbow to your right knee.

5. Continue alternating in this manner until you've completed all the recommended repetitions for each side.

Dos and Don'ts

✓ Make sure your entire upper-body torso is rotating during each rep, not just your elbow.

✗ A common mistake is rotating your hips on each rep. Your torso should be doing all the rotation. Remember to drive your legs straight out while keeping your lower back pressed into the floor for the entire set.

TIP: *If you feel a strain in your neck while doing this exercise, chances are you are pulling on your neck with your hands. Try doing the exercise with your fingers placed gently behind your ears.*

Try This!

CRUNCH: If bicycle crunches are too difficult, start with traditional crunches (page 73) and move to bicycle crunches when you need a challenge.

DUMBBELL SIDE BENDS: To change it up, do dumbbell side bends. Hold a dumbbell in one hand and bend toward that side. Allow the dumbbell to reach around knee level before using the opposite oblique to raise it back up, keeping the arm holding the dumbbell straight for the duration of the rep. Switch sides.

HOLLOW-BODY HOLD

Primary Muscles Involved: Abdominals

This exercise is a lot harder than it looks! It's one of the first exercises gymnasts learn and it involves bracing your abs and creating total-body tension. One of the benefits of this exercise is that it strengthens the entire abdominal region without putting your lower body at risk.

Instructions:

1. Lie on your back with your arms and legs extended.

2. Contract your abs, pulling your belly button toward the floor. Your arms and legs should be held straight out and your hands and toes pointed.

3. Slowly raise your legs and shoulders from the ground, followed by your arms and head. Your lower back must remain in contact with the floor.

4. Hold the position with your shoulders, arms, head, and legs raised off the ground for the duration of the set, and return to the floor with control.

Dos and Don'ts

✔ Practice! This exercise takes a little time to get used to. Once you get the hang of it, it is super effective. Keep your lower back pressed flat against the floor.

✖ While keeping your lower back pressed flat against the floor, don't allow space to form under the lower back. That is the key to this exercise.

TIP: *Begin with the arms and legs held higher from the floor (1 to 2 feet) and slowly develop strength until they can be held lower without compromising form.*

Try This!

LYING LEG-LIFT HOLD: This variation is similar to the hollow-body hold but you only lift your legs. While lying on the floor, keep your back pressed down and lift your legs 4 to 6 inches off the ground, keeping your legs straight. Hold the position and then slowly return your feet to the floor.

HANGING LEG RAISES: If you have access to a pull-up bar, hang from the bar and do leg raises.

CABLE PALLOF PRESS

Primary Muscles Involved: Abdominals (Obliques)

The cable Pallof press is probably the most deceptive exercise in the book. When you first look at it, it doesn't seem very difficult. In fact, you may even wonder why it's included. However, once you try it, prepare to be humbled.

Instructions:

1. Position a D-handle attachment to a cable pulley machine at about shoulder height.

2. Stand perpendicular to the cable machine and grab the handle with both hands. The handle should be in front of your body, with the resistance pulling to the side.

3. Step away from the tower so you are about an arm's length away from the pulley, keeping the weight's tension on the cable.

4. With your feet hip-width apart and knees slightly bent, pull the cable to the middle of your chest. This is your starting position.

5. Push the cable away from your chest, fully extending both arms. Your core should be tight and engaged.

6. Hold the rep for several seconds. Return to the starting position.

7. After a completed set, turn in the opposite direction and repeat the exercise for the other side.

Dos and Don'ts

✔ Stand with your knees bent, feet flat, and chest up to maintain a good position. Keep your shoulders down and back.

✘ The Pallof press is an anti-rotation exercise. Your hips and torso should not move during the exercise. The entire movement is predicated on maintaining a neutral spine and square hips.

TIP: *Brace your core hard. This is a good exercise to help reinforce full-body tension. You should be so tight that if one of the members of the gym ran into you, you would barely move.*

Try This!

BAND PALLOF PRESS: You can do the Pallof press with a thin resistance band secured around a pole, if you have one available.

KNEELING CABLE PALLOF PRESS: To make this exercise more challenging, do it from a half-kneeling position or a full kneeling position.

HOME WORKOUT HACK: *Side planks use the same muscles responsible for anti-rotation. Rotate onto your side with your bottom forearm flat on the floor and elbow lined up directly under your shoulder. Place the other arm on your hip. Both legs should be extended in a line, either staggered for more stability, or stacked for more of a challenge. Engage your core and lift your hips off the floor, forming a straight line from your head to your feet.*

LYING LEG LIFT

Primary Muscles Involved: Abdominals

If you're familiar with this exercise, whether from gym class or a workout video, your feelings about lying leg lifts are probably as conflicted as mine are from my days of wrestling practice in high school. But it's a great core exercise and, because you don't need any equipment, you can do them anywhere, anytime.

Instructions:

1. Lie on your back, flat on the ground, with your legs extended in front of you.

2. Place your hands on the floor by your hips. This is the starting position.

3. Keep your legs outstretched as straight as possible with your knees slightly bent but locked.

4. Raise your legs to a 90-degree angle from the floor and hold the contraction for 1 second.

5. Slowly lower your legs to the starting position. Control is everything; do not rush.

Dos and Don'ts

✓ For a more comfortable exercise, put your hands under your lower back/butt.

✗ It's very important that you do not arch your back. If you start to arch your back, it takes some of the tension off the abs so you aren't getting the full benefit of the exercise.

TIP: *If you want to make this exercise a little more challenging, raise your hips toward the ceiling when your legs are lifted.*

Try This!

LEG LIFT HOLD: To make the exercise easier, do leg lift holds instead of raises. To perform a leg lift hold, lift your legs and hold them about 6 inches off the ground for the designated time.

BENCH LYING LEG LIFTS: Do these on a bench, if one is available, instead of the floor. Performing the exercise on a bench makes the movement more difficult due to the greater range of motion, and because your legs don't rest on the floor at the end of each rep. All the same rules apply.

ARMS AND SHOULDERS

For many people, working on their arms and shoulders is all about appearance. Women frequently want "Michelle Obama arms" because hers are so beautifully toned and muscled. And men work toward rock-hard biceps. But there are functional reasons to strengthen your arms and shoulders. Every time you lift something, from a child to luggage to heavy tools or equipment, you need strong arms and shoulders. Developing these muscles will also help you avoid shoulder injury and increase and maintain flexibility in this crucial part of your body.

Most people instantly think of the biceps, but the upper arm also includes the triceps—and it's the triceps that actually make up the bulk of your arm. Biceps help control the movement of your elbow and shoulder, and triceps help you extend your arm and pull it back, and turn your forearm. You have three muscles in your shoulders, which you may have heard referred to as your delts. Each of these three muscles, the anterior deltoid, the middle deltoid, and the posterior deltoid, has its own function, so you'll need a wide range of exercises to develop your shoulders.

BAND PULL-APART

Primary Muscles Involved: Shoulder

The band pull-apart is simple yet effective. Although it is presented here as a warm-up exercise, the movement strengthens the muscles in your shoulders and upper back. By activating and engaging those muscles, your posture will improve, and you'll be able to press without pain. You need a resistance band to perform this exercise but they are fairly inexpensive and are a great investment for your home gym.

Instructions:

1. Begin with your arms extended straight in front of you, holding the band with both hands.

2. Initiate the movement by moving your hands out laterally to your sides, keeping your arms fully extended

3. As you perform the movement, bring the band all the way to your chest. That is the full range of motion.

4. When the band reaches your chest, pause for 1 second before returning to the starting position under control.

Dos and Don'ts

✓ Keep your wrists and elbows straight.

✗ This warm-up needs a slow, steady pace, so don't go too fast and/or shorten the range of motion.

TIP: *It's hard to do this exercise too much. If you ever feel like doing a little more at the end of your workout, do a couple of extra sets of band pull-aparts.*

Try This!

A LITTLE EASIER: If you need to build your strength as a beginner, use a lighter resistance band or take a wider grip on the band you are using.

A LITTLE MORE CHALLENGING: When you're ready for a challenge, use a heavier resistance band or take a narrower grip on the band you are using.

SEATED DUMBBELL SHOULDER PRESS

Primary Muscles Involved: Shoulder

This is a great exercise to prevent muscle imbalance or issues with stability while increasing strength across your shoulder region. Additionally, the exercise is done from a seated position so it creates less stress on your lower back.

Instructions:

1. Sit on a bench with a back support.

2. Hold two dumbbells at shoulder level, one on each side with an overhand grip and your palms facing forward. This is the starting position.

3. Press the dumbbells straight overhead.

4. When your arms are straight and fully extended, hold for 1 second, then return to the starting position.

Dos and Don'ts

✓ Only use a range of motion that is comfortable. If starting with the dumbbells at your shoulders is painful, start at ear level.

✗ Sometimes people have a tendency to lean back during this exercise, but by doing so you put your lower back at risk for injury, and you work some of the upper chest instead of keeping the focus on your shoulders.

TIP: *If you have a gym partner, ask them to help you get the dumbbells into the starting position. This can save you energy you can put toward the exercise.*

Try This!

LESS WEIGHT: If you need to start more slowly, use lighter weights.

ONE-ARM DUMBBELL SHOULDER PRESS: For a more difficult variation, either increase the weights or use one dumbbell at a time. The movement is performed the same way, except only one dumbbell is used.

HOME WORKOUT HACK: *If you don't have any weights at home, do the incline push-up position hold to work your shoulders. Get into the push-up position and elevate your feet on a box or other raised, flat surface. Aim to hold that position for a desired amount of time—15 to 20 seconds is an excellent place to start.*

DUMBBELL SIDE RAISE

Primary Muscles Involved: Shoulder (Lateral Delt)

If you've ever struggled to lift the garbage bag up and over into the garbage can, you can appreciate the need for this indispensable exercise. Nothing else will train the side part of your shoulder the way this exercise does, so be sure to include it in your program.

Instructions:

1. Stand with a straight back and your rib cage down, holding one dumbbell in each hand. (To bring your rib cage down, brace your core like you're getting ready for a punch.) This is the starting position.

2. Lead your sides until your arms are parallel to the ground.

3. Pause for 1 second before returning to the starting position.

Dos and Don'ts

✔ On the way up, tilt the dumbbell so the pinky comes up first. Your hand should make the motion of pouring a cup of water.

✘ A common mistake people make is shrugging their shoulders on the upward part of the movement. This takes some of the tension off the side delt and shifts it onto the trapezius muscle. Keep your shoulders retracted and locked down. The goal is to keep all the movement in the arms.

TIP: *To maintain the correct arm positioning, lead with your elbows, not your hands.*

Try This!

MACHINE LATERAL RAISE: If you just need to get the hang of this exercise, use a lateral raise machine at the gym. Sit down in the chair of the machine and place your elbows on the inside of the pads or rollers. Grab the handles, then contract your deltoids slowly to raise your arms up and out until they're parallel with the floor.

Keep your feet solidly on the floor and your back pressed against the chair. Return to the starting position.

SEATED DUMBBELL SIDE RAISE: Sit on the edge of a bench and do the movement exactly as described in the instructions.

HOME WORKOUT HACK: *If you have a resistance band, do banded side raises as a variation. Stand on the middle of the band, and holding the band at each side, perform the movement as described in the instructions.*

Y-W-T ISOHOLD

Primary Muscles Involved: Shoulder

The Y-W-T isohold is a great exercise to strengthen the shoulder and upper-back muscles. I love this exercise because it helps improve your posture. Most of us spend too much time sitting at our desks, or hunched over our phones, which causes our shoulders to round forward. The Y-W-T isohold strengthens the posture muscles to help reverse those effects.

Instructions:

1. Assume a prone (facedown) position on the floor or on a weight bench.

2. By flexing your shoulders and back muscles, hold your arms overhead in a "Y" position, not touching the floor or the weight bench. Hold this position for the desired time.

3. Next, lower your hands and elbows to create a "W" with your arms and head, again not touching the floor or the bench. Hold this position for the desired amount of time.

4. Lastly, move your hands out laterally to your sides to create a "T" position, not touching the floor or bench. Hold this for the desired amount of time.

Dos and Don'ts

✓ During the entire movement, aim to raise your arms as high as you can.

✗ This exercise requires your arms and hands to be lifted off the floor or bench, so don't allow them to rest on those surfaces.

> **TIP:** *Flex your shoulders and back during the entire exercise. Try to build as much tension as possible.*

Try This!

A LITTLE EASIER: To make the exercise easier, cut one of the positions. Instead of doing a Y-W-T isohold, just do a "Y-W" or a "W-T" isohold.

A LITTLE MORE CHALLENGING: When you're ready to progress, hold a light weight in each hand.

DUMBBELL HAMMER CURL

Primary Muscles Involved: Biceps

You've probably seen this exercise and know it works the biceps. What you may not realize is that it also strengthens your grip. With a stronger grip, you'll be able to carry in all the groceries with one trip! The neutral grip is important because it incorporates the brachialis, which is a muscle between your biceps and triceps. This makes the dumbbell hammer curl one of the best all-around bicep exercises.

Instructions:

1. Stand erect, holding two dumbbells, one on each side, using a closed, neutral grip (palms facing your body). Position the dumbbells along your thighs with your arms fully extended. This is the starting position.

2. Keeping the dumbbells in a neutral grip, curl them toward your shoulders. Pay attention to the position of your elbows. Your elbows should remain steady at your side throughout the entire rep. Avoid letting them drift forward during the movement.

3. Once executed, lower the weights until your elbows are fully extended.

Dos and Don'ts

✓ Squeeze the dumbbell as hard as you can during the movement. This will help improve your grip strength.

✗ If the weight is too heavy, it's common for the elbow to drift forward or out to the sides during the rep. This takes the tension off the biceps and shifts it to the shoulders. You want to lock the elbow in place for the duration of the set, so you may need to use a lighter weight.

TIP: *To focus more on each arm, perform one arm at a time.*

Try This!

BARBELL CURL: If hammer curls are too difficult at first, start with a traditional barbell curl. To do a barbell curl, take an underhand grip on a barbell and curl the weight up toward your shoulders.

REVERSE CURL: For a more difficult alternative, try a reverse curl. To perform the reverse curl, grasp a barbell with a reverse or pronated grip: Grasping it with your palms facing your body; when you curl the barbell up to your shoulders, your palms will face outward. This will incorporate more forearm than a traditional curl.

BENCH DIP

Primary Muscles Involved: Triceps

The bench dip is one of the simplest and most effective triceps exercises. It's also a great transition into regular parallel bar dips. This is also one of the more versatile exercises in the book with multiple ways to make it easier or more challenging.

Instructions:

1. Sit on a bench and grip the edge with your hands. Scoot your butt off the bench and walk your feet out in front of you until your knees are not bent, your weight is on your heels and your hands, and your arms are straight. This is your starting position.

2. Slowly lower your body by bending your elbows, stopping when your upper arms are parallel to the floor and your butt is a few inches off the ground.

3. Using your triceps, lift your torso to the starting position.

Dos and Don'ts

✓ If you have any shoulder pain, limit the range of motion.

✗ Keep your hips as close to the bench as possible and don't let them shift away from the bench. Keeping your torso upright will help.

TIP: *Keep your elbows as close to your body as possible throughout the movement.*

Try This!

CABLE TRICEPS PRESSDOWN:
If the bench dip is too difficult to start with, an easier triceps exercise variation is the simple cable triceps pressdown. This is a basic movement that allows you to start with a light weight to build up your strength to, eventually, move to the bench dip. Start with a high cable attachment and press the weight down while keeping your elbows tucked in at your sides.

FEET-ELEVATED BENCH DIP: To make the exercise more difficult, place your feet up on another bench instead of the ground. Beyond that, place a weight plate on your lap to add more resistance.

> **HOME WORKOUT HACK:** *This exercise can easily be done at home. Instead of using a bench, use a sturdy and stationary chair, couch, or desk to place your hands on.*

DEAD HANG

Primary Muscles Involved: Shoulder, Forearm

With this one relaxing stretch, you'll improve your shoulder health, range of motion, and grip strength as well as decompress your spine. The dead hang is great for loosening the entire shoulder region with the help of gravity. If grip strength is a limiting factor at first, keep your feet on the ground and only apply as much weight/pressure as you can hold.

Instructions:

1. Grip an overhead bar with an overhand grip and with your hands about shoulder-width apart. Relax the whole body, specifically reducing tension in your shoulders and lower back.

2. Keep your arms straight. Just relax and hang.

Dos and Don'ts

✓ If your gym allows it, put a little chalk on your hands before doing this exercise, which will make it easier to grip the bar.

✗ To get the greatest benefit from the exercise, don't contract your shoulder muscles. Allow the shoulders to relax and let go of any tension in the lats. Imagine you're lengthening your body as much as possible.

TIP: *Use any grip you want—overhand, underhand, neutral grip, etc.—whichever grip feels the most comfortable for your shoulders.*

Try This!

LAT PULLDOWN STRETCH: If your grip or strength doesn't yet let you do the dead hang, the lat pulldown machine will get you started. You won't have gravity helping, but you can add enough weight to get the same kind of stretch. All the same rules apply: Relax your shoulders and get a good stretch.

ONE-ARM DEAD HANG: If the standard dead hang is not challenging enough, try doing it with only one hand at a time. This will place a huge demand on your grip strength, but it can really help with shoulder stability if you are able to build up the strength to complete the movement.

HOME WORKOUT HACK: *You'll get so many great benefits from doing a dead hang that I recommend buying a doorway pull-up bar. Starting your day with a dead hang will get you loosened up and off to a good start.*

CHEST

Although professional body-builders focus on developing their chest muscles, in part, for aesthetic value, working your chest muscles will have a great benefit in your daily life. Your chest muscles are some of the largest muscles in your upper body and you use them all day long. They are responsible for moving your arms across your body and for pushing; anytime you push open a door, wash your hair, or get up and down from the floor, you're using your chest muscles. Women sometimes mistakenly think this training is less important for them than for men, but these muscles are important for posture and breathing and they support your shoulder blades and shoulder joints, so having strong chest muscles can help you avoid injury in those areas, in addition to all the rest.

The pectorals are a muscle group with multiple attachment points, so you need a variety of angles and exercise variations to work them effectively. Simple adjustments, such as bench angle, can affect the area of the muscle that is most stimulated by an exercise. For example, compared to a flat bench press, an incline bench press shifts more focus toward the upper chest.

BAND DISLOCATION

Primary Muscles Involved: Shoulder

You could do this exercise every day to loosen your shoulders. When you're preparing for a chest workout, it's especially important to do this warm-up exercise to avoid injury. It will warm and loosen your shoulders and get them moving. Shoulder injuries are common and starting a chest workout without a warm-up is asking for trouble.

Instructions:

1. Hold the ends of a light resistance band in each hand. Begin with the band in front of your torso with your hands down at your sides.

2. Stretch the band slightly to increase the tension. Your hands should be wider than shoulder-width apart.

3. While keeping your shoulder retracted and arms straight, begin to raise the band overhead and back down behind you.

4. Once you come to the end of the range of motion, return to the starting position.

Dos and Don'ts

✓ Try to move your shoulders through the greatest range of motion you can safely perform.

✗ Throughout the entire range of motion, it's important to keep constant tension on the band, pulling out all the slack. Don't release the tension on the band.

TIP: *Do this exercise slowly and focus on getting a good stretch.*

Try This!

ARM CIRCLES: If the band dislocations are a little too difficult to start with, perform the same range of motion without the bands.

NARROW GRIP BAND DISLOCATIONS: As you get stronger, grab the band with a narrower grip to increase tension.

HOME WORKOUT HACK: *You can also do this movement with a broomstick or a long PVC pipe.*

PUSH-UP

Primary Muscles Involved: Chest

Although this one might make you groan, the push-up is a valuable tool in your training program. An unusual thing about this exercise is that it's one of the only chest exercises that keeps your scapula, or shoulder blade, free to move. Push-ups are effective for building upper-body strength, but they also engage the core and can strengthen your lower back. Because women tend to have less upper-body strength than men, it's an important exercise in a woman's program.

Instructions:

1. Lie facedown on the floor and place your hands on either side of your shoulders. With the balls of your feet touching the floor, fully extend your arms to lift your torso.

2. Lower yourself until your chest almost touches the floor, making sure to keep your core tight.

3. Push up with your arms again, lifting your upper body to the starting position.

Dos and Don'ts

✅ Screw your hands into the ground to create more shoulder stability. This will help prevent injury and improve performance.

❌ Your glutes and abs should be tight and your body should be in a relatively straight line throughout the entire movement. Don't allow your hips to sag and touch the ground or raise up to create an arch. If you are having trouble with this, try squeezing your glutes during the movement.

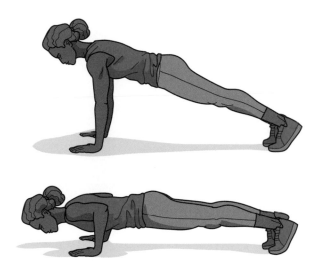

TIP: Put a book or foam block under your chest to give you a goal of touching your chest to the book or block during each rep.

Try This!

HAND-ELEVATED PUSH-UP: If you struggle to do a normal push-up, try hand-elevated push-ups. This is simply a push-up with your upper body elevated and your hands placed on a bench or the pin of a power rack. As the push-ups become easier, progressively lower your hand elevation.

WEIGHTED PUSH-UP: When regular bodyweight push-ups become too easy, add resistance by wearing a weight vest or having someone put a weight plate on your back.

BARBELL BENCH PRESS

Primary Muscles Involved: Chest

The bench press is probably my favorite exercise, and one that has greatly benefited me. The bench press can be a very safe lift—if done correctly—and is responsible for more upper-body muscle growth and strength than any other exercise. As with any exercise, if done *incorrectly* the bench press can be problematic, so take the time to learn proper form. **SAFETY NOTE:** Anytime you put weight over your head, use a spotter.

Instructions:

1. Lie on a flat bench and position yourself so your eyes are below the racked bar.

2. Before grasping the bar, arch your back, and squeeze together your shoulder blades. Think about trying to hold a pencil in your upper back. Not only is this the most effective way to bench press the most weight, it is also the safest. Use your legs to help drive your upper back into the bench.

3. Once you are set, grasp the bar with an even grip slightly wider than your shoulders.

4. Lift the bar out of the rack and position it over your chest, with your arms fully extended. This is the starting position.

5. Take a deep breath, brace your core, and lower the bar to touch your chest at about the level of the nipples.

6. After a brief pause, push the bar back to the starting position. Focus on pushing the bar up and slightly back toward the rack.

7. Once you are back at the starting position, hold for 1 second, then start the next rep.

8. When you are done, place the bar back in the rack.

Dos and Don'ts

✅ It's very important to lower the weight slowly toward your chest—with control. You may have seen people bouncing the bar upward when it reaches their chest. This increases the risk of injury and decreases the chest activation.

❌ It's common to see people letting their butts come off the bench during the rep, which can lead to back pain and lessens the effectiveness of the exercise. Imagine pushing your toes through the front of your shoes, which will help keep your butt on the bench.

TIP: *This is an important case where the dimensions of your body make a difference. Longer arms need a wider grip. Try different grip widths until you find the placement that's right for you.*

Try This!

SMITH MACHINE BENCH PRESS:
If you struggle with balancing the bar when bench pressing, using a Smith machine can be helpful. A Smith machine has a fixed barbell that moves along a vertical "track." Because the bar is fixed in place, you don't have to balance the weight.

SLOW-TEMPO BENCH PRESS:
For a challenge, take 5 seconds to lower the weight to your chest.

HOME WORKOUT HACK: *The best at-home alternative to the bench press is the push-up.*

INCLINE DUMBBELL BENCH PRESS

Primary Muscles Involved: Chest

The incline dumbbell bench press shifts the focus to the upper chest, near your collarbone. It allows for both sides of the chest to be worked at the same time, preventing one side from getting bigger than the other. The incline dumbbell bench press is my favorite incline variation to use for the upper part of the chest because the barbell press tends to be hard on the shoulders. Adjust the bench angle to find what works best for you. Use an angle less than 45 degrees, if available.

Instructions:

1. Sit on the edge of a flat or inclined bench with a dumbbell in each hand, resting on top of your knees. Your palms should face each other.

2. Use your knees to help kick up the dumbbells. Lift them one at a time so you can hold them at shoulder level.

3. Rotate your wrists forward so your palms face away from you. This is the starting position.

4. To begin the movement, push the dumbbells up to full arm extension.

5. Once you reach full extension, slowly lower the weights to the starting position.

Dos and Don'ts

✓ One benefit of using dumbbells is the greater range of motion they allow. However, because there is no definitive end point as there is with a barbell bench press, it's easy to cut the rep short. Make sure you always use a full range of motion unless an injury causes you to do otherwise.

✗ If you arch your back too much, it takes the tension off the upper chest and defeats the purpose of the exercise. It's okay to have your shoulders retracted, but try to limit excessive arching.

TIP: *If it feels more comfortable, press the dumbbells straight up with a neutral grip (palms facing each other) instead of using a pronated grip, facing away from you.*

Try This!

INCLINE HAMMER STRENGTH MACHINE PRESS: This is an easier variation to work the upper-chest region, as you don't have to worry about stabilizing the dumbbells. With this exercise, all you have to do is adjust the seat, sit down, and press.

RING PUSH-UPS: If you have access to a set of gymnastics rings or a TRX device, ring push-ups are one of the best push-up variations, and also an excellent variation to the dumbbell bench press.

HOME WORKOUT HACK: *If you have a set of dumbbells at home but no bench, do a dumbbell floor press. Lie on the floor holding the dumbbells and press them up. You won't have the full range of motion, but the floor press is effective on its own.*

DUMBBELL PULLOVER

Primary Muscles Involved: Chest, Lats

Bodybuilders use this exercise to bulk up their chest muscles, leading it to become synonymous with Arnold Schwarzenegger's physique. It's a shame it seems to have fallen out of style with more recreational weight lifters, because in addition to getting you pumped up, it's easy on the elbows and works the lats and serratus.

Instructions:

1. Stand a dumbbell vertically on a flat bench for easy reach.

2. Lie perpendicular on the bench with only your shoulders and upper back on the surface. Your head should be off the bench, your hips should be below the bench, and your legs should be bent. Plant your feet firmly on the floor.

3. Hold the dumbbell with your palms pressing the underside of the top weight. Slightly bending your arms, raise it above your chest. This is your starting position.

4. While keeping your bent arms locked in the starting position, slowly lower the weight in an arc behind your head until you feel a good stretch across your chest.

5. At that point, bring the dumbbell back, in the same curving motion, to the starting position.

Dos and Don'ts

✓ Get a good stretch in the bottom position—really try to "open up" your rib cage.

✗ If you bend your arms too much the exercise works your triceps more than your chest and lats. Keep the same arm angle throughout.

> **TIP:** *As you pull up the dumbbell, flex the chest hard at the top.*

Try This!

PULLOVER MACHINE: If this exercise is a bit too challenging, and your gym has a pullover machine, try this alternative, but understand it focuses on the lats a little more than the chest. Adjust the seat so your arms are flat on the pads. Reach above and grab the bar. Drive your arms and elbows into the pads as you pull the bar down as far as the machine will allow. Slowly return the weight to the starting position.

EZ BAR PULLOVER: You can also use an EZ bar instead of a dumbbell for pullovers. The EZ bar allows you to lift more weight, which can make the exercise more challenging.

CABLE CROSSOVER FLY

Primary Muscles Involved: Chest

The cable crossover fly is a great exercise to work the chest muscles with a different movement pattern than pressing. When you look at chest anatomy, the muscle fibers run horizontally from the sternum to the shoulders. During a dumbbell fly, when the dumbbells are at the top, the weight is resting mostly on the bones and joints, taking tension off the muscle. A fly motion allows the chest muscle fibers to stretch fully during each rep. During a cable crossover, there is an equal amount of tension throughout the entire range of motion, which leads to more muscle activation.

Instructions:

1. Start by placing two pulleys in a high position on opposite sides of the cable station.

2. Grab a pulley in each hand. Center yourself between the pulleys while drawing your arms together in front of you. Your torso should bend slightly forward from your waist. Keep your feet in a split stance with one foot in front of the other. This is your starting position.

3. With only a slight bend in your elbows, extend your arms to the sides in a wide arc until you feel a stretch across your chest.

4. Once your arms stretch back as far as they can, return to the starting position, using the same arcing motion to lower the weights.

5. Hold for 1 second at the starting position, then repeat.

Dos and Don'ts

✓ Keep your elbows locked in one position throughout the entire range of motion.

✗ If you use too much weight, there will be a tendency to press the weight instead of "fly" the weight in an arc movement pattern.

TIP: *Changing the pulling angle from high to low and everything in between can modify the effect of the exercise. Experiment with different angles to find the one you like best.*

Try This!

PEC DECK: If your gym has a pec deck machine, this movement is very similar to a cable crossover and is a little easier to master because it moves along a fixed plane. With the pec deck, adjust the seat, sit down, and move the handles toward each other in a fly movement pattern.

DUMBBELL FLY: If you want a slightly more demanding exercise, a dumbbell fly is a good alternative. Lying on a flat bench with a dumbbell in each hand, raise them above your chest with your palms facing each other. With a slight bend of your elbows, lower your arms out at both sides in a wide arc, until you feel a stretch in your chest. Return your arms to the starting position.

DOORWAY CHEST STRETCH

Primary Muscles Involved: Chest

I love a stretch that can be done anywhere—and this is a great one. Maintaining a good range of motion is important to avoid injury, and this cooldown stretch really opens your chest and shoulders. It's great to do at the end of an upper-body workout.

Instructions:

1. To perform the stretch, stand next to a doorway with a staggered stance and extend your right arm horizontally, in line with the floor.

2. Place your right hand on the doorway and turn your body away from your arm. Concentrate the stretch on the right pectoral and hold it.

3. Repeat on the left side.

Dos and Don'ts

✓ Move your hand higher or lower on the doorway to change the focus of the stretch until you find the area that is tight.

✗ When performing this stretch, you don't need your arm fully extended. In fact, maintaining a slight elbow bend can allow for a better stretch.

TIP: *By turning your body away from the stretching side, you increase the intensity of the stretch.*

BEHIND-THE-HEAD CHEST STRETCH: A great alternative to the doorway stretch is the behind-the-head chest stretch. To perform the stretch, place your hands behind your head with your fingers interlocking. From there, pull your elbows back behind your ears and hold the stretched position.

WEIGHTED DUMBBELL STRETCH: For a more challenging stretch, hold two dumbbells, one in each hand, in the bottom position of a dumbbell bench press and use the weight to stretch the chest. When finished, lower the weights to the ground.

PART THREE

PUTTING IT ALL TOGETHER: 4 WEEKS OF WEIGHT LIFTING ROUTINES

HERE IS WHERE the fun begins! In the coming pages you will find a complete four-week weight lifting routine with three workout days per week. This is designed to help you get your weight lifting journey started on the right foot. The program includes warm-up and cooldown exercises to be performed each training day, along with a list of beginner-friendly exercises. Adhere to the sets and reps provided to make sure you're not doing too much too soon.

As you will notice, there is built-in progression within the four weeks. In Week 1, you will perform two sets of each exercise and, by Week 4, you build to three sets of each exercise.

I recommend keeping track of how much weight you use on each exercise. (See page 5 for some recommended ways to track your lifting.) Your goal is to try to lift heavier weights—with good form— each week.

THE DAILY WARM-UP AND COOLDOWN CIRCUITS

The daily warm-up exercises and cooldown stretches will be the same for every workout.

The Warm-Up

General warm-up: 5 minutes of light cardiovascular activity (walking, exercise bike, elliptical machine, etc.)

Specific warm-up:

1. Air Squat (page 36): 2 sets of 8 to 10 reps

2. Rope Lat Extension (page 52): 2 sets of 8 to 10 reps

3. Band Dislocation (page 100): 2 sets of 8 to 10 reps

4. Band Pull-Apart (page 84): 2 sets of 8 to 10 reps

The Cooldown

1. Hurdle Stretch (page 48): 2 sets per side, with a 15- to 20-second hold on each side

2. Lat Stretch (page 64): 2 sets per side, with a 15- to 20-second hold on each side

3. Doorway Chest Stretch (page 114): 2 sets per side, with a 15- to 20-second hold on each side

4. Dead Hang (page 96): 2 sets, with a 10- to 30-second hold

WEEK 1

The first week of any new workout program is the hardest. The most important thing is to develop good habits and consistency—whether going to the gym or doing the workout at home. If you complete all three workouts this week, it's a big win!

I want you to focus on doing all the exercises correctly and with good form. This is just the beginning. Don't be in a rush to see how much weight you can lift. There will be plenty of time in coming weeks to increase the amount of weight you are using.

Day 1

1. Dumbbell Goblet Squat (page 38): 2 sets of 6 to 8 reps

2. Dumbbell Step-Up (page 42): 2 sets of 6 to 8 reps

3. Seated Cable Row (page 58): 2 sets of 8 to 10 reps

4. Incline Dumbbell Bench Press (page 107): 2 sets of 8 to 10 reps

5. Cable Crossover Fly (page 112): 2 sets of 8 to 10 reps

6. Dumbbell Hammer Curl (page 92): 2 sets of 10 to 12 reps

7. Weighted Decline Sit-Up (page 70): 2 sets of 10 to 12 reps

8. Rope Cable Crunch (page 72): 2 sets of 10 to 12 reps

9. Lying Leg Lift (page 80): 2 sets of 10 to 12 reps

Note: Remember to do your warm-up and cooldown exercises!

Day 2

Rest Day

There are four rest days each week, which are important both physically and psychologically. Fitness is best when it adds to your life, not when it takes over your life. Use your rest days as an opportunity to do other hobbies or activities outside the gym.

Day 3

Muscle soreness is going to be high this week, as your body adapts to the new demands placed on it. Don't worry! It will get better—hang in there. To mitigate some of the soreness, take a hot bath when you get home from the gym today.

1. Barbell Bench Press (page 104): 2 sets of 6 to 8 reps

2. Seated Dumbbell Shoulder Press (page 86): 2 sets of 6 to 8 reps

3. Barbell Romanian Deadlift (page 40): 2 sets of 6 to 8 reps

4. Dumbbell Lunge (page 46): 2 sets of 8 to 10 reps

5. Dumbbell Row (page 56): 2 sets of 8 to 10 reps

6. Y-W-T Isohold (page 90): 2 sets of 10-second holds in each position

7. Plank (page 68): 2 sets of 30-second holds

8. Bicycle Crunch (page 74): 2 sets of 10 to 12 reps

9. Cable Pallof Press (page 78): 2 sets of 10 to 12 reps

Day 4

Rest Day

Look good, feel great, perform well.

Okay, hear me out. One of my favorite things to do when starting a new training program is to buy new workout clothes. It's almost the same idea as when you were a kid and couldn't wait for the first day of school to wear your new outfits! Not only will you be more excited to go to the gym (and wear your new workout clothes) but, if you look and feel good, you are on your way to a great workout. If you don't need any new clothes, grab some new gym shoes!

Day 5

Congratulations! You've made it through the first week of exercises. Starting anything new, like a new workout program, is a challenge. I always tell my clients that getting through the first week is the hardest. Finish out the week strong!

1. Lat Pulldown (page 54): 2 sets of 6 to 8 reps

2. Inverted Row (page 60): 2 sets of 6 to 8 reps

3. Dumbbell Bulgarian Split Squat (page 44): 2 sets of 6 to 8 reps

4. Push-Up (page 102): 2 sets of 8 to 10 reps

5. Dumbbell Pullover (page 110): 2 sets of 8 to 10 reps

6. Dumbbell Side Raise (page 88): 2 sets of 8 to 10 reps

7. Bench Dip (page 94): 2 sets of 8 to 10 reps

8. Back Extension (page 62): 2 sets of 10 to 12 reps

9. Hollow-Body Hold (page 76): 2 sets of 10 to 30 second holds

Days 6 and 7

Rest Days

This first weekend is going to be critical! Keep your momentum going and stay active these two rest days. Make it a game to see how many 10-minute walks you can take, or make it a point to go for a bike ride. Take your fitness outside and enjoy some fresh air. Appreciate your new approach to self-care and focus on ways you might treat yourself! You might consider something physical, like getting a massage, or social, like involving friends or your partner in fun activities, or something like getting a manicure or another kind of professional grooming treat.

WEEK 2

Awesome work! You made it through the first week and now you're ready to build on what you accomplished in Week 1. Before moving on to Week 2, review your notes. Take a look at how much weight you used for each exercise the previous week. The goal is to try to use a little more weight this week—even if it's only 5 pounds more. Progression is the name of the game!

Note that the first three exercises of each workout now include three sets instead of two.

Day 1

1. Dumbbell Goblet Squat (page 38): 3 sets of 6 to 8 reps

2. Dumbbell Step-Up (page 42): 3 sets of 6 to 8 reps

3. Seated Cable Row (page 58): 3 sets of 8 to 10 reps

4. Incline Dumbbell Bench Press (page 107): 2 sets of 8 to 10 reps

5. Cable Crossover Fly (page 112): 2 sets of 8 to 10 reps

6. Dumbbell Hammer Curl (page 92): 2 sets of 10 to 12 reps

7. Weighted Decline Sit-Up (page 70): 2 sets of 10 to 12 reps

8. Rope Cable Crunch (page 72): 2 sets of 10 to 12 reps

9. Lying Leg Lift (page 80): 2 sets of 10 to 12 reps

If you aren't sure you're doing an exercise with correct form, take a video of yourself and compare it to the visuals in part two.

Day 2

Rest Day

Rest days provide the perfect opportunity to do the little things outside of the gym that help further your weight lifting journey. Something as simple as going to the grocery store and making sure you have the right food for healthy meals is critical to your long-term success. Refer to page 12 for some snack ideas that will keep you full and help you get the most out of your workouts.

Day 3

If any exercise in this workout routine is too challenging, or even too easy, use the alternatives listed in part two.

1. Barbell Bench Press (page 104): 3 sets of 6 to 8 reps

2. Seated Dumbbell Shoulder Press (page 86): 3 sets of 6 to 8 reps

3. Barbell Romanian Deadlift (page 40): 3 sets of 6 to 8 reps

4. Dumbbell Lunge (page 46): 2 sets of 8 to 10 reps

5. Dumbbell Row (page 56): 2 sets of 8 to 10 reps

6. Y-W-T Isohold (page 90): 2 sets of 10-second holds in each position

7. Plank (page 68): 2 sets of 30-second holds

8. Bicycle Crunch (page 74): 2 sets of 10 to 12 reps

9. Cable Pallof Press (page 78): 2 sets of 10 to 12 reps

Day 4

Rest Day

Making fitness part of your life doesn't just happen in the gym, or during your workout. There are many ways to track our daily steps, which is a great measure of your overall activity. Most smartphones come with an app that tracks your steps and you can find others that track steps and other aspects of your activity. A general guide is to take between 8,000 and 10,000 steps each day.

Day 5

As you come to the conclusion of Week 2, remember that a majority of the exercises can be modified to do at home. If you miss a day at the gym, you can still get quality work done at home.

1. Lat Pulldown (page 54): 3 sets of 6 to 8 reps

2. Inverted Row (page 60): 3 sets of 6 to 8 reps

3. Dumbbell Bulgarian Split Squat (page 44): 3 sets of 6 to 8 reps

4. Push-Up (page 102): 2 sets of 8 to 10 reps

5. Dumbbell Pullover (page 110): 2 sets of 8 to 10 reps

6. Dumbbell Side Raise (page 88): 2 sets of 8 to 10 reps

7. Bench Dip (page 94): 2 sets of 8 to 10 reps

8. Back Extension (page 62): 2 sets of 10 to 12 reps

9. Hollow-Body Hold (page 76): 2 sets of 10 to 30 second holds

Days 6 and 7

Rest Days

Swimming is an excellent activity to do on your rest days. Not only is it low impact, which spares your joints, it's also a great form of active recovery to help prepare you for Week 3 of your new weight lifting program! If swimming isn't an option, investigate new activities that will keep you moving and motivated. Perhaps there are yoga classes in your area, or even Tai Chi classes.

WEEK 3

Now that you have two weeks' experience, you should be feeling more comfortable with the exercises.

There is huge value in getting better at performing the movements. Lifting weights is a skill and, like any skill, you get better at it with practice. This is one reason the exercises remain the same for the duration of the four weeks.

Motivation alone, along with the excitement of doing something new, probably pushed you through the first two weeks. Over the years, I have found the third week is where things get a little tougher. Make it a point to keep the consistency going. This is the week to get over the hump. Once you make it past Week 3, you are more likely to keep going.

Notice, the first six exercises of each workout now have three sets instead of two.

Day 1

As the dumbbell goblet squat is the first exercise of the day, it's the one you want to focus on improving the most, week to week.

1. Dumbbell Goblet Squat: 3 sets of 6 to 8 reps (page 38)

2. Dumbbell Step-Up (page 42): 3 sets of 6 to 8 reps

3. Seated Cable Row (page 58): 3 sets of 8 to 10 reps

4. Incline Dumbbell Bench Press (page 107): 3 sets of 8 to 10 reps

5. Cable Crossover Fly (page 112): 3 sets of 8 to 10 reps

6. Dumbbell Hammer Curl (page 92): 3 sets of 10 to 12 reps

7. Weighted Decline Sit-Up (page 70): 2 sets of 10 to 12 reps

8. Rope Cable Crunch (page 72): 2 sets of 10 to 12 reps

9. Lying Leg Lift (page 80): 2 sets of 10 to 12 reps

Day 2

Rest Day

Take a *literal* rest day today! Take a nap. Extra sleep is one of the best things to improve how quickly and how well you recover from your workouts. Use the time you are normally at the gym to take a quick 15- to 20-minute nap. Or, go to a neighborhood park and do some people watching, or cloud watching. Give yourself permission to do absolutely nothing for 20 minutes.

Day 3

I know this may sound cliché, but focus on what you can control—attitude and effort. That goes for every exercise, not just the bench press. It's easy to get sidetracked by what others do in the gym, or what you see on social media. Everyone responds to training differently. Have confidence in yourself and aim to improve each week.

1. Barbell Bench Press (page 104): 3 sets of 6 to 8 reps

2. Seated Dumbbell Shoulder Press (page 86): 3 sets of 6 to 8 reps

3. Barbell Romanian Deadlift (page 40): 3 sets of 6 to 8 reps

4. Dumbbell Lunge (page 46): 3 sets of 8 to 10 reps

5. Dumbbell Row (page 56): 3 sets of 8 to 10 reps

6. Y-W-T Isohold (page 90): 3 sets of 10-second holds in each position

7. Plank (page 68): 2 sets of 30-second holds

8. Bicycle Crunch (page 74): 2 sets of 10 to 12 reps

9. Cable Pallof Press (page 78): 2 sets of 10 to 12 reps

Day 4

Rest Day

If you tried a yoga class on a previous rest day, either take another class or explore other types of yoga! There are many types—from restorative yoga to hot yoga. If one doesn't catch your interest, another just might. Take a friend or your partner with you, and do something fun together afterward.

Day 5

You have probably noticed that some days you feel better than others. This is perfectly normal. Nutrition, sleep, stress, and other lifestyle factors play a role in our gym performance. On days you feel good, push yourself a little more. On days you don't, it's okay to just match what you did the previous week and go home.

1. Lat Pulldown (page 54): 3 sets of 6 to 8 reps

2. Inverted Row (page 60): 3 sets of 6 to 8 reps

3. Dumbbell Bulgarian Split Squat (page 44): 3 sets of 6 to 8 reps

4. Push-Up (page 102): 3 sets of 8 to 10 reps

5. Dumbbell Pullover (page 110): 3 sets of 8 to 10 reps

6. Dumbbell Side Raise (page 88): 3 sets of 8 to 10 reps

7. Bench Dip (page 94): 2 sets of 8 to 10 reps

8. Back Extension (page 62): 2 sets of 10 to 12 reps

9. Hollow-Body Hold (page 76): 2 sets of 10 to 30 second holds

Days 6 and 7

Rest Days

The end of Week 3 is a great time to analyze your progress. How have you been doing? Be honest. With only one week left, this is a perfect time to refocus and finish out the last week strong. What has gone well? Where have you struggled? If you've had trouble staying motivated, think about ways you can help push through those moments, whether that's problem solving or making an accountability arrangement with a friend.

WEEK 4

Although this is the last week of the four-week program, this is really just the beginning. My goal is for you to take what you have learned from these initial four weeks and build upon it for the rest of your life. Weight lifting is an activity you can do for a long time. As long as you are smart and stay injury free, lifting weights is the fountain of youth. Notice that exercises in each workout now have three sets.

Day 1

Plan ahead—the workouts may take a little longer to complete because there are three sets for every exercise this week.

1. Dumbbell Goblet Squat (page 38): 3 sets of 6 to 8 reps

2. Dumbbell Step-Up (page 42): 3 sets of 6 to 8 reps

3. Seated Cable Row (page 58): 3 sets of 8 to 10 reps

4. Incline Dumbbell Bench Press (page 107): 3 sets of 8 to 10 reps

5. Cable Crossover Fly (page 112): 3 sets of 8 to 10 reps

6. Dumbbell Hammer Curl (page 92): 3 sets of 10 to 12 reps

7. Weighted Decline Sit-Up (page 70): 3 sets of 10 to 12 reps

8. Rope Cable Crunch (page 72): 3 sets of 10 to 12 reps

9. Lying Leg Lift (page 80): 3 sets of 10 to 12 reps

Day 2

Rest Day

You have done such a great job so far and you deserve to treat yourself as a reward. Get a massage! Maybe it's time for a haircut or manicure or a professional shave by a barber. You've put a lot of effort into taking care of yourself, so expand that to your appearance. If you find your clothes are fitting a little differently, try on some new clothes—whether you buy them or not. This can be a good way to *see* the effect of your hard work.

Day 3

As this is the last week of the program, try to hold a plank for longer than 30 seconds on the last set.

1. Barbell Bench Press (page 104): 3 sets of 6 to 8 reps

2. Seated Dumbbell Shoulder Press (page 86): 3 sets of 6 to 8 reps

3. Barbell Romanian Deadlift (page 40): 3 sets of 6 to 8 reps

4. Dumbbell Lunge (page 46): 3 sets of 8 to 10 reps

5. Dumbbell Row (page 56): 3 sets of 8 to 10 reps

6. Y-W-T Isohold (page 90): 3 sets of 10-second holds in each position

7. Plank (page 68): 3 sets of 30-second holds

8. Bicycle Crunch (page 74): 3 sets of 10 to 12 reps

9. Cable Pallof Press (page 78): 3 sets of 10 to 12 reps

Day 4

Rest Day

If you have equipment at home, go through the warm-up and cooldown routine on rest days as a form of active recovery. Doing the stretches can be a way to relax at the end of the day and keep your muscles warm and flexible.

Day 5

On the last set of inverted rows, aim to do as many bodyweight reps as possible with good form.

1. Lat Pulldown (page 54): 3 sets of 6 to 8 reps

2. Inverted Row (page 60): 3 sets of 6 to 8 reps

3. Dumbbell Bulgarian Split Squat (page 44): 3 sets of 6 to 8 reps

4. Push-Up (page 102): 3 sets of 8 to 10 reps

5. Dumbbell Pullover (page 110): 3 sets of 8 to 10 reps

6. Dumbbell Side Raise (page 88): 3 sets of 8 to 10 reps

7. Bench Dip (page 94): 3 sets of 8 to 10 reps

8. Back Extension (page 62): 3 sets of 10 to 12 reps

9. Hollow-Body Hold (page 76): 3 sets of 10 to 30 second holds

Days 6 and 7

Rest Days

Use this weekend to find a new workout program to follow, or get ready to start this program again. You now have enough experience and knowledge to evaluate new programs, or investigate gyms, if you've completed this program at home. Take a moment to acknowledge that you have grown and taken an important step toward your long-term health and strength, and you aren't where you started.

I hope you received what you wanted from this book. Ultimately, it's what you do after these four weeks that is most important. Ideally, this is the start of a lifelong journey. We live in an amazing time. Take advantage of the opportunity to learn and expand your weight lifting knowledge. You're in control now!

Resources

Here is a list of resources to help you continue progressing in your weight lifting journey.

WEBSITES

Hunt Fitness: www.kylehuntfitness.com

I provide hundreds of free articles, podcasts, interviews, and videos about weight lifting. I also offer one-on-one online coaching if you want to take the next step in your fitness journey.

Rogue Fitness: www.roguefitness.com

Rogue Fitness, the industry leader in American-made strength and conditioning equipment, is the place for almost everything you could need for workouts, including squat racks, barbells, knee sleeves, belts, shoes, and more.

The Absolute Strength Podcast: www.kylehuntfitness.com/category/podcast

On this podcast, I answer questions and interview some of the biggest names in the fitness industry. Find it on my website or iTunes, Stitcher, Google Play, YouTube, and Spotify.

BOOKS

Delavier, Frédéric. *Strength Training Anatomy*. Champaign, IL: Human Kinetics, 2006.

A great book if you want to dive deeper into human musculature and anatomy.

Starrett, Kelly, and Glen Cordoza. *Becoming a Supple Leopard: The Ultimate Guide to Resolving Pain, Preventing Injury, and Optimizing Athletic Performance* 2nd ed. Las Vegas, NV: Victory Belt Publishing, 2015.

This is an excellent book to learn more about mobility and soft tissue work. To make progress, you have to keep your body healthy.

Glossary

abdominal muscles: The series of muscles located on the front of the body, on the lower midsection of the torso.

active recovery: The act of performing low-intensity/low-effort exercise following a hard workout. Active recovery is typically done on a rest day.

arm muscles: The arm muscles consist of the biceps and triceps. The biceps are the flexor muscles located on the front of the upper arms. The biceps are responsible for bending the hand toward the upper arm. The triceps are the extensor muscles of the upper arm. The triceps work in opposition to the biceps. The triceps are responsible for extending the lower arm.

back muscles: The entire group of muscles located on the back side of the upper-body torso. The back muscle complex includes the latissimus dorsi, spinal erectors, trapezius, rhomboids, and teres minor and major.

barbell: A barbell consists of a long bar, collars, sleeves and associated plates. Barbells can be adjustable (allowing plates to be added or taken off) or fixed (the barbell is a nonadjustable weight).

bodyweight exercise: Any exercise that uses your own bodyweight for resistance.

cable machine: A machine with long wire cords attached to weight stacks at one end and a handgrip at the other.

cardiovascular/aerobic exercise: Any activity that increases the body's need for oxygen by using large muscle groups continuously.

chest muscles: The large chest muscles, also called pectoral muscles, are located on the front of the upper torso and are responsible for drawing the arms forward and in toward the center of the body.

circuit: A series of exercises done back to back with a relatively brief rest between each exercise.

compound exercise: Any exercise that works more than one muscle group at a time; examples include the squat and bench press.

dehydration: The state in which the body has insufficient water levels for proper functioning.

DOMS (delayed onset muscle soreness): Muscle discomfort that appears 12 to 48 hours after lifting weights.

dumbbell: Short bars on which weight plates are fixed and secured. Dumbbells can be considered a one-arm version of a barbell. Most dumbbells have the weight written on their side.

flexibility: Range of motion possible at a joint, or the ability to use joints and muscles through their full range of motion.

frequency: Can refer to how often a movement is trained per week, how often a muscle group is trained per week, or how often a workout is performed per week.

glute muscles: Also known as the buttocks, the glute muscles consist of the gluteus maximum, medius, and minimus. The glutes comprise one of the strongest muscle groups in the human body and are responsible for moving the hips and thighs.

isolation exercise: Any exercise aimed at working one muscle group at a time, such as a biceps curl or leg extension.

leg muscles: Consist of the quadriceps, the large muscles located on the front side of the upper legs responsible for extending the lower leg forward, and hamstrings, which are located on the back of the upper legs and are responsible for curling the foot toward the upper leg.

muscular endurance: The ability of the muscle to perform repetitive contractions over a prolonged period of time.

muscular strength: The ability of the muscle to generate the maximum amount of force.

program: Another word for routine, schedule, plan, etc., referring to the complete number of sets, reps, and exercises performed on a given day.

progressive overload: The gradual increase of stress placed upon the body during training.

proper form: The specific way of performing an exercise to avoid injury, prevent cheating, and increase effectiveness.

range of motion (ROM): The measurement of movement around a specific joint or body part. A full range of motion refers to the maximum amount of movement around a specific joint for a given exercise.

recovery: The process of returning to a pre-exercise state.

rep: Short for "repetition," referring to one complete movement of an exercise, such as squatting and standing back up, which is one rep.

rest period: The amount of time between each set of an exercise, typically, 1 to 3 minutes.

set: The performance of a group of consecutive reps in a row.

shoulder muscles: Also called the deltoid muscles, these consist of the anterior, middle, and posterior deltoids. The deltoid muscles are located at the top of the torso and are responsible for elevating and rotating the arms.

stretching: A form of exercise for which the primary goal is increased flexibility.

training log/training journal: Notebook or app used to keep track of exercises, weight, sets, reps, energy, etc.

training to failure: Continuing a set until the muscle simply cannot contract to complete any additional reps.

weight plate: Varying sizes of circular iron weights placed on the barbell to add weight. Weight plates typically come in 2½ pounds, 5 pounds, 10 pounds, 25 pounds, 35 pounds, and 45 pounds.

References

Gordon, Brett R., Cillian P. McDowell, Mats Hallgren, et al. "Association of Efficacy of Resistance Exercise Training with Depressive Symptoms: Meta-Analysis and Meta-Regression Analysis of Randomized Clinical Trials." *JAMA Psychiatry* 75, no. 6 (June 2018): 566–576. doi:10.1001/jamapsychiatry.2018.0572.

Harris-Fry, Nick. "Bicycle Crunches: The Best Abs Exercise According to ACE." June 4 2019. *Coach*, www.coachmag.co.uk/exercises/lose-weight/1716/bicycle-crunches.

Layne, Jennifer E., and Miriam E. Nelson. "The Effects of Progressive Resistance Training on Bone Density: A Review." *Medicine & Science in Sports & Exercise,* 31, no. 1 (1999): 25–30. doi:10.1097/00005768-199901000-00006.

Ma, Tongyu, and Chong Lee. "Associations of Healthy Lifestyle Behaviors with Cardiovascular Disease and Chronic Disease Mortality and Life Expectancy in Men and Women." *Medicine & Science in Sports & Exercise* 48, 5S Supplement 1 (May 2016): 554. doi:10.1249/01.mss.0000486665.35632.92.

O'Connor, Patrick J., Matthew P. Herring, and Amanda Caravalho. "Mental Health Benefits of Strength Training in Adults." *American Journal of Lifestyle Medicine* 4, no. 5 (July 2010): 377–396. doi:10.1177/1559827610368771.

Index

Weight machines, 7, 19, 22, 30
Weight plates, 8
Wide-Grip Seated Cable Row, 59
Workout gear, 21–22, 119
Workout journals/logs, 5
Workout routines

basic elements, 8–9
four-week routine, 116–126

Y

Yoga, 123
Y-W-T Isohold, 90–91

Acknowledgments

Like every endeavor of my life, this book was the result of many helping hands. First, I would like to thank my wife, Ashlyn, and my daughter, Lucille. Writing two books in one calendar year was challenging, and I thank you for being patient and supportive.

I forgot to properly acknowledge my mom in my first book, so I want to make sure I don't make that mistake again! In all seriousness, I want to give a huge thank you to my mom and my stepdad. Without you guys there is no way I would be who I am today. Thank you for all the rides to the gym when I was a kid—I told you it was going to lead to something!

Next up is the entire team at Callisto Media. I can't thank you guys enough for giving me the opportunity and making this project come to fruition.

Lastly, I would like to thank all the clients with whom I have had the opportunity to work over the years. I have learned so much from them the past 10-plus years. At the end of the day, there is no substitute for real-world experience.

About the Author

Kyle Hunt is a competitive powerlifter, coach, author, and owner of Hunt Fitness, a highly sought-after online fitness and nutrition coaching business. Kyle specializes in building workout and nutrition programs customized to individual goals. He has worked with hundreds of clients, including bodybuilders, physique athletes, powerlifters, wrestlers, and clients from all walks of life—all aiming to be their best. Kyle has a bachelor of science degree in exercise science from Fredonia State University and is a certified fitness trainer and fitness nutrition specialist.